W9-AGM-280

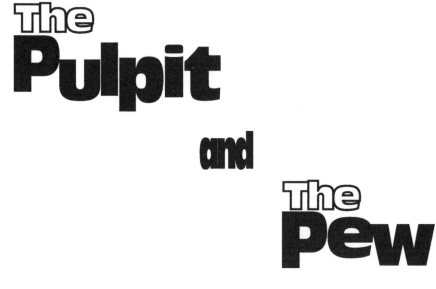

The Pulpit and The Pew

Discussions on conflict in the Lord's house

Bishop Marshall Gilmore

The and The
Pulpit Pew

Discussions on conflict in the Lord's house

Bishop Marshall Gilmore

The Pulpit and The Pew

Copyright © 1997 by The CME Publishing House
Published in the United States of America
CME Publishing House
William E. George, General Secretary
4466 Elvis Presley Blvd.
Memphis, Tennessee 38116

All rights reserved.

No part of this book may be reproduced or transmitted in any form or
by any means, electronic or mechanical, including photocopying and
recording, or by any information storage or retrieval system without
permission from the publisher.

Scripture quotations, unless otherwise indicated, are from the New
Revised Standard Version of the Bible, copyright © 1989 by the
Division of Christian Education of the National Council of Churches
of Christ in the United States of America and are used by permission.
All rights reserved.

Library of Congress Cataloging-in-Publication Data
Gilmore, Marshall
The Pulpit and The Pew:
Discussions On Conflict In The Lord's House/Marshall Gilmore
ISBN 1-883667-19-4
1. Pulpit — Ordained. 2. Pew — Unordained. 3. Church — Conflict.

97-71253
LCCCN

Published by The CME Publishing House
Memphis, Tennessee, United States of America

CONTENTS

Chapter V

PULPIT UNDER ATTACK

Types of attackers

PROLOGUE

This volume, *Pulpit And Pew, discussions on conflict in the Lord's house*, is the author's attempt to verbalize some of the conditions affecting community among the people of God in Christ. The reader, it is hoped, will see in the several vignettes some of their own experiences and involvements. And from reading find, both, some answers that are workable in their situations and where needed provide incentives for individuals to change, or to become agents of change.

Running through this book is the belief that God's intention for creation is community. In a proximate way the church reflects and represents that community. Within the church are friends and foes of community. Pulpit, my way of speaking of the Pastor, is positioned as the leader of Pew, my way of referring to members, individually and collectively. This approach takes seriously the several gifts bestowed by the Spirit upon the ordained and the unordained for ministry. From the mix of gifts Pulpit is set apart and not above for oversight of the entire congregation. Pew is called to ministry but is not given oversight of the whole people of God in that one place.

Pulpit and Pew are members of the body of Christ and together are responsible for maintaining its unity. My prayer is that all of us will become more intentional in our concern for the negative influences and effects of conflict. Likewise, I pray that our resolve to act will be strengthened.

Rev. William E. George, General Secretary of the Department of Publications, the Christian Methodist Episcopal Church encouraged me to "write something." While he was not specific on what to write, I chose this topic, and hope not only that Rev. George will be pleased but that many will be helped. So, I am grateful to him and to my wife, Yvonne Dukes Gilmore, whose patience and perseverance with me as I use so much time at home writing evidence grace. Our daughter Joan Gilmore-Oglesby always encourages me in my writing ministry; to her I am grateful. Earlier in another endeavor I mentioned our son John Marshall with whom I bounce ideas back and forth. Some break. Others hold.

Ms. Debra Ann Kimble of Shreveport, Louisiana, my former secretary, has mastered deciphering my arthritic affected handwriting, so I owe her a great deal of thanks for typing and retyping this manuscript. Finally, I am grateful to my present secretary, Karla Mays-Thomas for her help in taking on some of my tasks in order to free up some of my time for us in completing the writing.

Yours in the ministry of Christ!

Marshall Gilmore
Presiding Bishop
8th Episcopal District
C.M.E. Church
Dallas, Texas

Chapter I
PULPIT AND PEW HAVE THINGS
IN COMMON

Pulpit and pew share a common calling. God called them by the same grace. *One*, by His justifying grace, He made all creation right with Himself. He sent Jesus His only Son into the world out of a stunningly different kind of love. He proves just how unique His love is, for in our sinful state and for our sinful deeds, Christ came among us and died for us. All creation, nature and human, are justified before God. Justification is God's benevolence in Jesus the Christ by whose death made right the past, present, and future of all creation. He forgave all sins and washed away all guilty stain. No one could do it, except God. All things in heaven and on earth were made by Him and belong to Him. He is the owner of all things. John got it right when he says, "All things came into being through him, and without him not one thing came into being" *(John 1:3)*. Paul reminds us that all things were "created ... for him" *(Col. 1:16)*. So all things are made for God. When sacred things, human and non-human, animal and nature, are violated God is violated. David knew as much and revealed it in his confession. After committing adultery with Bathsheba, whose husband he also had killed, David confessed, "For I know my transgressions, and my sin is ever before me. Against you, you alone, have I sinned, and done what is evil in your sight" *(Ps. 51:3, 4a)*. All sin is against the righteousness of the Holy God. The scribes were technically, if not spiritually, correct and proper when they questioned in their hearts, "Who can forgive sins but God alone?" *(Mk. 2:7b)*. The righteous God to whom all things belong has forgiven sin. His will and may I say God's heart-desire is to "come to have first place in everything" *(Col. 1:18b)*. From Sinai onward when God said, "You shall have no other gods before me" *(Exod. 20:3)*, He made explicit what was implicitly said to Adam in the garden of Eden *(Gen. 2:16-17)*. Father Adam disobeyed God causing a great divide between creation and Creator. But as Paul says, "through *(Christ)* God was pleased to reconcile to himself all things, whether on earth or in heaven, by making peace through the blood of his cross" *(Col. 1:20)*.

The "God who justifies" *(Rom. 8:33)*, justified the world in Jesus of Nazareth, the Anointed One. Through the blood of Jesus God pronounced creation righteous. But there is a catch. In the catch is a challenge. The catch is the world has been saved and will not acknowledge it. Its war against right and righteousness is over and God won. But the world is in denial. It refuses to acknowledge defeat. In its state of denial, business as usual continues. The world moves today on the same presuppositions that Reinhold Niebuhr noted more than forty years ago. The two presuppositions are, one, the perfectibility of the human specie; and, two, the idea of progress. The first does not take the universal presence of sin seriously. Thus, its contaminating effects upon all that human beings set their mind and hand to are not adequately assessed. The human ego and its will to power, even to the extent of playing God or thinking itself to be God is universal. Moving side by side and/or in tandem with the concept of human perfectibility, which does not take sin seriously, is belief in progress. A belief that combines education as the means for overcoming shortcomings in the human family with the conviction that science and technology through their breakthroughs and advancements will bring in world community.

The Christian point of view is that, "all have sinned and fall short of the glory of God" *(Rom. 3:23)*. The noblest of human efforts and achievements have within them the Tower of Babel Syndrome. "Come, let us build ourselves a city, and a tower with its top in the heavens, and let us make a name for ourselves" *(Gen. 11:3)*.

On the surface the efforts to build a city and a tower seem harmless indeed. Upon closer examination, however, the motives are suspect. Of primary importance in this regard is the motive, "let us make a name for ourselves." Of course the means for doing so was the building of a city and a tower. Nonetheless, these seem harmless activities. Except, they reflect a shift from dependency upon God to dependency upon themselves and their own initiatives. The top of the tower they would build would be "in the heavens." God's domain would be invaded. Humankind by its own initiative would "be like God" *(cf. Gen. 3:15)*, which is humankind's primary sin. To be like God means not only being without God, but it means also having no need for God. The God of the Bible is a jealous God. He refuses to accept the worship of other gods *(Exod. 20:3)*. Where universal human sin and concomitant evil are denied and the theory of progress embraced, it is easy to see how generations have "exchanged the truth about God for a lie and worshipped and served the creature rather than the Creator" *(Rom. 1:25)*.

The Christian challenge is to go to the world and let it know that it is accountable to God *(Rom. 3:19)*. God has justified it and He did so as its Creator with every right to do so. In the face of the world's certainty of building permanently, the Church must let it know, "the world and its desires are passing away, but those who do the will of God live forever" *(I John 1:17)*. The inclination of the world is to claim finality for what it does. However, finality cannot be claimed for its work is seen. Only the unseen is eternal *(II Cor. 4:18)*. Further, in as much as all humankind is guilty of sin, and only God is holy and righteous, the works of humankind are contaminated.

So, again, the challenge to the Christian Church, pew and pulpit is to go into the world and say to it, "You are justified!"

Second, Pulpit and Pew, pastor and people are members of the one body of Christ." Through the water of rebirth and renewal by the Holy Spirit" *(Titus 3:5)*, both are initiated into Christ's body. God who is no respecter of persons in the world, "he makes his sunrise on the evil and on the good, and sends rain on the righteous and on the unrighteous" *(Matt. 5:45)*, does not condone preferences in His Church. Baptized members are clothed with Christ in whom, "There is no longer Jew or Greek, there is no longer slave or free, there is no longer male and female; for all of you are one in Christ Jesus" *(Gal. 3:28)*.

Just in case I was not clear earlier, all who are members of the body of Christ share God's saving grace *(Eph. 2:8-9)*. Many different expressions are used to describe it, "He touched me"; "He washed me"; "He shook my dungeon and my chains feel off"; "He redeemed me"; "He fixed me"; "He saved me." All refer to the work of God's saving grace, personally experienced. Justification is a thing done by God for all creation. Regeneration is when God's general or universal act of justification becomes God's grace for me. Each person who is saved or born again has received a personal dose of grace. No matter what we think of Thomas, he did not accept what other disciples said regarding the Resurrected Christ. He had to see Jesus for himself. Once Thomas was satisfied that this was the same man who answered his question, "Lord, we do not know where you are going. How can we know the way?", saying, "I am the way, and the truth and the life" *(John 14:5-6)*, Thomas cried, "My Lord and my God" *(John 20:28)*.

All who acknowledge that Jesus is Lord belong to him and to one another. Paul wrote, "we, who are many are one body in Christ, and individually we are members one of another" *(Rom. 12:5)*. Preacher and people are bound together one with the other in a bond of divine grace. Our unity and oneness is not by denominational name, it is not by local church name. It may manifest itself in these human institutions and structures. But its primary source is "one Lord, one faith, one baptism, one God and Father of all" *(Eph. 4:5)*.

Unity is not only God's nature, He wills it for creation. The Trinity is the Church's way of expressing God's unity. Jesus commanded his disciples to baptize in the trinitarian "name of the Father and of the Son and of the Holy Spirit" *(Matt. 28:19)*, which means a coming "into" relationship with the Lord.

Pulpit and Pew, pastor and people are baptized members of the one body of Christ. We all got there by the same means. "For in the one Spirit we were all baptized into one body ..." *(I Cor. 12:13)*. What we must be careful to remember, always, is that we do not create the body. We enter it. Even that is not by our works. We are drawn into it. If you will, we are called into it, "called to be saints, together with all those who in every place call on the name of our Lord Jesus Christ, both their Lord and ours" *(I Cor. 1:2b)*. The words of Paul were addressed to a local church in Corinth. He emphasizes the fact that the Christians, or "saints," as he called them, were so called in unity with all others in every place who recognized Jesus as Lord. That recognition today unifies all of the saints everywhere in one body.

What responsibility does each saint have to maintain unity? I suggest Paul's instructions to the Church at Ephesus "to maintain the unity of the Spirit in the bond of peace" *(Eph. 4:3)*, are instructive for us. This exhortation says, first, there is a unity which the Spirit creates. And, second, saints or disciples of Christ are responsible for keeping the unity by working for harmony in relationships.

So maintaining unity is the responsibility of each and every member. Since the Church is God's people in Christ, to break unity or impair it is to do damage to Christ himself. The Church is the body of Christ. Too often we do not think of the Church in this way. From that perspective, local churches are little more than human institutions or organizations. They are not regarded as sacred or of divine origin. Nonetheless, the Church is of God. He purchased it with the blood of Jesus the Christ. From the New Testament it is clear that the local church is the Church of God. Paul's Letter "to the church of God that is in Corinth" was written to a local congregation. "The Greek word for church is *"ekkleesia,"* from the preposition *ek*, meaning "from"; and the verb *"kaleoo,"* "to call out." A church is a group of people called out of the world, while still living in the world, for a witness to the world for the Lord. This is its general universal meaning."[1]

Every local church is the Church of God. All of its members are responsible for maintaining the unity in the Spirit. The point of departure for doing so is self.

---

[1]Spiros Zodhiates. *A Richer Life For You in Christ* (Chattanooga, TN, AME Publishers, 1972), p. 18f.

Remember Jesus said that if you are at the altar offering your gift and it hits you that a member has something against you, it is your duty to find that person and get the relationship right *(Matt. 5:21-26)*.

The other side of this matter is the responsibility of the offended.   Christians who have been offended by another member of the Church is to forgive. By forgiving others an offended saint will be forgiven by our heavenly Father *(Matt. 6:14-15)*.

The unity and oneness of the Church is so important until Jesus provided for reproving a member who sins against another. His system is designed to "save" the offender. A three-pronged process beginning with the offended member going to the offender, if that does not work, one or two other members are to be taken, if that does not work, the offender is to be taken before the whole Church. "If the offender refuses to listen even to the church, let such a one be to you as a Gentile and a tax collector" *(Matt. 18:15-20)*.

While the purpose of the judicial process outlined by Jesus is to regain a wayward member, even its harshest penalty, putting a member out, is intended to maintain unity. Dissensions that are divisive causing ruptures in the Church impair the spirit of unity.

Third, Pulpit and Pew enjoy the benefits of God's sanctifying grace. Every Christian's patron saint ought to be the man who told Jesus, "I believe; help my unbelief" *(Mk. 9:24)*. Sanctification has to do with the areas of "unbelief" in believers. All of us who are saved, I maintain, are kindreds of the man referred to above. Of course there are some pious souls who claim to "have no doubt." God bless them! But I stick by my position that all believers are in the boat with the man who had "unbelief." Where total unwavering belief exists, you will find complete trust also. The two are inseparable twins. Sweet is the soul's peace where trust is maturing. Made for God, human beings are comforted and consoled when their souls rest trustingly in God. But, where are the Christians with "complete trust" in God?

Sanctification is God's grace working with believers to conform them more and more after the image of Christ. In order for us to grow into his image, we must have in us the mind of Christ *(Philp. 2:5)*. The mind Christ had in himself allowed him to let God be first *(Philp. 2:6)*. He willed to be one with God in will and work *(cf. John 4:24; 6:38)*. "Being born in human likeness" *(Philp. 2:7)*, Jesus went through testing to arrive at the point where he said, "Abba, Father, ... yet, not what I want, but what you want" *(Lk. 14:36)*.

Some may not like the thought of Jesus growing in faith, but it is a critical part of my belief system. If he is my example of what God intends us to be, then, he must grow into the example because I am not there. Moreover, except Jesus struggled to get where he got he does not know what it means to struggle. I submit to you I am confident that I am on solid ground in this matter. The Letter To The Hebrews speaks thusly about the matter:

> *In the days of his flesh, Jesus offered up prayers and supplications, with loud cries and tears, to the one who was able to save him from death, and he was heard because of his reverent submission.*
>
> *Although he was a Son, he learned obedience through what he suffered; and having been made perfect, he became the source of eternal salvation for all who obey him, having been designated by God a high priest according to the order of Melchizedek.*
> Heb. 5:7-10

Christ in believers helps them in their weaknesses to become perfected in God. He is able to do this because, "Jesus," himself, "increased in wisdom and years, and in divine and human favor" *(Lk. 2:52)*. It would be difficult for some of us to feel an affinity with Jesus if his testing was not real and served no real purposes. The words of the Holy Scriptures would be mockery, which say, that Jesus was a great high priest "who in every respect has been tested as we are, yet without sin" *(Heb. 4:15)*, if the testing could not have had a different outcome.

Jesus dealt with the tempter in the wilderness by resisting him. At the heart of the three temptations, like in every temptation, was choice and decision making. By the choices we make, as was true with Jesus, growth takes place. In the way of God, choices that pull us out of ourselves into the service of others and the glory of God are sanctioned by Him. What Jesus resisted in the wilderness, namely, self-serving and self glorifying and self aggrandizing opportunities were later congealed in another opportunity and another like response. "When Jesus realized that they were about to come and to take him by force to make him king, he withdrew again to the mountain by himself" *(John 6:15)*.   Ultimately decisions relate to vocation when vocation is understood in the New Testament sense of "salvation," which itself is wholeness or health of being.   Jesus' temptations were about work, his work, thus, God's work.   So are ours.   Work is not life defining.   We bring meaning to work when we have our lives together.   That's what Jesus did.   He got his life together in preparation for doing God's work.

Fourth, Pulpit and Pew share a common humanity. They are born in time and they die in time.   In between the womb and the tomb believers all have a heavenly treasure in earthen vessels.   It is the nature of the vessels that make sanctification necessary.   Preacher and people have flesh and blood to war against.   In other words, we found the enemy and the enemy is us.   It is our own flesh and blood that is at war with our spirit.   Paul spoke of the war going on in "my members."   Doing good was opposed by evil which "lies close at hand" *(Rom. 7:21-25)*.   Rescue from the conflict, however, is at hand.   "Who will rescue me from the body of this death?   Thanks be to God through Jesus Christ our Lord!"   If God's victory in Jesus Christ is to be realized in any of us, we must allow it.   We must declare a truce between the mind to which Paul said, "I am a slave to the law of God" and the flesh to which the apostle also said, "I am a slave to the law of sin" *(Rom. 7:25b)*.

If the mind and not the flesh is to have mastery in the soul, we must "lay aside every weight and the sin that clings so closely" *(Heb. 12:1)*.   Conscious and intentional efforts must be made to think right in order to develop a right spirit from which right actions follow.

Jesus counseled, thus, "Either make the tree good, and its fruit good; or make the tree bad, and its fruit bad; for the tree is known by its fruit.   You brood of vipers! How can you speak good things, when you are evil?   For out of the abundance of the heart the mouth speaks.   The good person brings good things out of a good treasure, and the evil person bring evil things out of an evil treasure" *(Matt. 12:33-35)*.

Between birth and death, being Christian is about becoming more like Jesus the Christ.   It is about making the heart or the mind good so that good may come from it. I suggested earlier that right thinking ought to be practiced until it becomes habitual.   That which occupies the heart will come out.   It has been said quite well, I submit, that the true beliefs of any of us are not what we say but what we practice. Again, it is out of the heart that true behavior comes. Individuals who are overtly pious in worship on Sunday morning have been known, for no obvious reasons, to behave disruptively in business meeting on Monday night. On second thought, could the same emotional source be behind both types of behavior?

Regardless of the negatives associated with our humanity, God created us human. David, referring to human beings said, "You have made them a little lower than God, and crowned them with glory and honor" *(Ps. 8:5)*. The human being is in a very privileged position because of God's image. With privilege, however, is responsibility. Christian church members "have clothed yourselves with the new self, which is being renewed in knowledge according to the image of the creator" *(Rom. 3:10)*. Knowledge according to the image of the creator embraces a sense of unity and oneness amidst diversity in the body of Christ, where, "Christ is all and in all!" *(Rom. 3:11)*.

The earthen vessels housing the heavenly treasure can be improved upon. That is the work of sanctifying grace. Where Jesus' challenging command is heeded, "Be perfect, therefore, as your heavenly Father is perfect" *(Matt. 5:48)*, God's Spirit is at work within to bring us to the level where we love without regard for whether or not we are loved *(cf. Matt. 5:43-47)*. Constantly we must stay near the potter's house. There God's grace is available for reshaping every part of us that is not growing toward perfection in love *(cf. Jer. 18:1-4)*.

Paul's Letter To The Colossians include instructions calling for personal actions that are both negative and positive. Negative in the sense of taking some things out of our lives. "Put to death, therefore, whatever in you is earthly: fornication, impurity, passion, evil desire, and greed *(which is idolatry)* ... These are the ways you also once followed, when you were living that life. But now you must get rid of such things -- anger, wrath, malice, slander and abusive language from your mouth. Do not lie to one another, ..." *(Col. 3:5, 7, 8, 9a)*.

Cleaning out, getting rid of and sweeping clean make only one part of the equation. That is the human approach to religion. We stop doing something. All or many negative doings are discontinued. What one has is

not bad, it results in good ethics. But a risk is set up--one
that Jesus reminded us of. He told what happens when an
unclean spirit has gone out of a person and wanders about
through waterless regions looking for a resting place, find
none, decides to return to its former house. The person
from whom the spirit left is now swept clean and in order
and empty. The unclean spirit who is still unclean goes
and brings seven other spirits more evil than itself. "And
the last state of that person is worse than the first" *(cf. Luke
11:24-26)*.

On the positive side, Paul advises, "clothe
yourselves with compassion, kindness, humility, meekness,
and patience. Bear with one another and, if anyone has a
complaint against another, forgive each other ... Above all
clothe yourselves with love, ..." *(Col. 3:12, 13, 14)*.

Can human beings do these things by themselves?
If so, does it mean that they have completed what I
referred to as "good ethics"? From a humanistic approach,
individuals may successfully cease and desist certain
behaviors and begin a commendable and noble lifestyle.
But from a Christian point of view every human being has

a heart disease that can be corrected only by a heart transplant *(Jer. 24:7)*.

It is important for us to keep before us the fact that the people to whom Paul wrote "have died, and your life is hidden with Christ in God" *(Col. 3:3)*. They were, "God's chosen ones" *(3:12)*. They had experienced heart transplants. What they were called upon to do they did not have to do alone. Once saved it became a partnership. As Paul put it, "I can do all things through him who strengthens me" *(Philp. 4:13)*.

Christians have their being in a rather precarious position. Through the Lord Jesus Christ they "have obtained access to this grace in which we stand" *(Rom. 5:1-2)*. With all of the freedom we have from being in Christ, how are we to behave? We have access to forgiving grace, so what do we do? Paul answered, thus, "Should we continue in sin in order that grace may abound? By no means! How can we who died to sin go on living in it?" *(Rom. 6:1-2)*. Christians cannot use their humanity as an excuse for sinning. They have died to sin.

Fifth, Pulpit and Pew are gifted for ministry by the same God. Since all gifts are from God, they are what He wills for everyone of us.

I will go beyond, as far as I am able to tell, what the Pauline writings mean by the distribution of gifts. What I will do is use gifts as presented in Ephesians 4:7-16 given to the Pulpit or the Pastor. And the gifts in I Corinthians 12:1-21 will be directed generally to mean the Pew, or to the people. The hinge on which this interpretation turns is Ephesians 4:11a and 12, namely, "The gifts he gave were ... to equip the saints for the work of ministry, for building up of the body of Christ."

Callings, positions, offices in the Church are God given. In I Corinthians 12:7-11, it is through the Spirit that the several manifestations are bestowed. They are given to maintain unity, or as Paul notes, "for the common good." On the other hand, Ephesians 4:11 attributes to Christ the giving of the gifts.

Gifts differ "according to the grace given to us" *(Rom. 12:6)*. Does that make Pulpit and Pew, pastor and people different? I say not. Paul admonished the Romans, saying, "For by the grace given to me I say to everyone among you not to think of yourself more highly than you ought to think, but to think with sober judgment, each according to the measure of faith that God has assigned" *(Rom. 12:3)*.

What is different among the gifts is function. All the members of the Church "do not have the same function" *(Rom. 12:4)*. Because every gift is an act of God there is no basis for bragging or boasting or gloating.

Yet, my position is that the gifts given to the Pulpit or pastor are given to equip the Pew or the people for ministry. It is important for the well-being of the Church that each part works properly. When that is being done, the body grows spiritually and numerically *(Eph. 4:16)*.

In the local church, the pastor is gifted to equip officers and members for ministry. While some may limit the gifts to those listed in the New Testament, I maintain that the Church conscious of and committed to its reason for being is within its scope of prerogatives when it names as ministries its several offices and functions. The Christian Methodist Episcopal Church, for example, would do well to regard Steward, Stewardess, Trustee, Director of Christian Education and Minister of Music, etc., as ministries which God gifts individuals to fulfill.

When the office of deacon was instituted in the apostolic church, it resulted to meet a service need. Why should today's church not have the same right? *(cf. Acts 6:1-7)*. I would counsel any church to be as circumspect in doing so as was the disciples. They called the whole community of disciples together and shared the need with them. The community chose seven men for whom the apostles prayed and laid their hands upon.

The establishment of the office of deacon added a ministry in the division of church labor. The deacons set apart would work "in the daily distribution of food." The twelve disciples called apostles said we "will devote ourselves to prayer and to serving the word" *(Acts 6:1a, 4)*. So within the apostolic fellowship there were divisions of labor.

Paul wrote some things that address multi-ministries. One, I Corinthians 12:14-20 speaks to what I call covetousness. The apostle uses body parts foot and hand, eye and ear to make his point. For example, he says, "If the foot would say, 'Because I am not a hand, I do not belong to the body' that would not make it any less a part of the body."

No matter how a particular ministry is regarded in church structure, either by those who hold the position or those who stand without and judge it, God established the arrangement. Paul said, "But as it is, God arranged the members in the body, each one of them, as he chose" *(I Cor. 12:18)*.

The other thing spoken to in I Corinthians 12:20-26 is individual *arrogance*. Expressed in Paul's words, "The eye cannot say to the hand, 'I have no need of you, nor again the head to the feet, 'I have no need of you.'" Where dissension exists in a congregation among church officers, remember the question, "If all were a single member, where would the body be?" *(I Cor. 12:19)*.

I Corinthians 12 deals with gifts as given for the common good. That is made known in the words where Paul talks of mutual care, or "the same care for one another. If one member suffers, all suffer together with it; if one member is honored, all rejoice together with it" *(I Cor. 12:25-26)*.

Pulpit or pastor has a different ministry. A ministry different from the Pew or people. It is an equipping ministry. A ministry given to build up the Pew or people for their ministries. Given the tendencies in some ecumenical circles to blur the lines between Pulpit and Pew, I emphatically declare there is a difference. The primary distinction is *functions*. But difference in expectation, especially of the Pulpit, exists, also.

Ezekiel a prophet of the Lord reminded Israel's shepherds that they were expected to place the welfare of the sheep above their own. Falling short of what the Lord expected, feeding themselves, and not taking care of the needs of the sheep, the Lord said, "no longer shall the shepherds feed themselves. I will rescue my sheep from their mouths, so that they may not be food for them" *(cf. Ezek. 34:1-10)*.

Jeremiah zeroed in on the cause behind the shepherds insensitivity and their shirking of responsibility. He said in the Lord's name, "the shepherds are stupid and do not inquire of the Lord; therefore, they have not prospered and their flock is scattered" *(Jer. 10:21)*. In his own defense Jeremiah said, "I have not run away from being a shepherd in your service" *(17:16)*.

God places pastors in positions to shepherd the people. Consider what shepherds did not do according to Ezekiel. "You have not strengthened the weak, you have not healed the sick, you have not bound up the injured, you have not brought back the strayed, you have not sought the lost, but with force and harshness you have ruled them" *(Ezek. 34:4)*. Greater responsibility requires stricter accountability. "From everyone to whom much has been given, much will be required; and from the one to whom much has been entrusted, even more will be demanded" *(Lk. 12:48b)*.

The Book of Ritual of the Christian Methodist Episcopal Church in the ordination of elders shows just how serious the office is taken. In the outset, ordinands are told, "Have always in your remembrance how great a treasure is committed to your charge. For they unto whom you are to minister are the sheep of Christ, for whom he gave his life."[2]

---

[2] Bishop Marshall Gilmore, editor (C.M.E. Publishing House, Memphis, 1995), p. 119.

The exhortation to seriousness is followed by a warning which represents accountability. "And if it shall happen the church, or any member thereof, do take any hurt or hinderance by reason of your negligence, you know the greatness of the fault."[3]

The Christian Methodist Episcopal Church maintains in charge language relative to the Pew, or the pastor. Ordinands in waiting for hands to be laid upon them, setting them apart as elders, are told: "Wherefore see that you never cease your labor, your care, and your diligence until you have done all that lieth in you, according to your bounded duty, to bring all such as shall be committed to your charge unto perfectness in Christ."[4]

Ministries differ but all are derived from the one ministry of Christ. His ministry is the ministry of reconciliation, which God effected through him. I return to my discussion of justification, which I described as God's finished work of redemption *(cf. John 19:30)*. Paul used the English translated past tense "reconciled" to

---

[3]Ibid. p. 119f.

[4]Op. cit., p. 120.

describe God's work in Christ *(II Cor. 5:18)*, which suggests again God's "finished" work. On the basis of God's finished work of reconciliation, He "has given us the ministry of reconciliation" *(II Cor. 5:18)*. Pulpit and Pew, pastor and people have been given the same ministry. All are entrusted with "the message of reconciliation" *(19b)*. According to the ministry of each individual "the message of reconciliation" is to be shared. While the Pulpit or pastor preaches the message in a setting of corporate worship, the Pew or people do their spreading of the message in different settings and in different ways.

I am always moved and instructed by Jesus' approach to doing ministry. So often he took the available opportunity and met it appropriately. If I may without being held to strict interpretation for correctness, Jesus' ministry was broad enough in scope to encompass and symbolize the work of Pulpit and Pew. He proclaimed the good news of the kingdom of God from city to city *(Lk. 4:43)*. By chance, if you will, "he was in one of the cities, there was a man covered with leprosy," and he cured him *(Lk. 5:12-16)*. One day while teaching, he healed a paralytic *(Lk. 5:17b)*. He fed the hungry *(Lk. 9:10-20)*. He visited with friends, Martha and Mary, where he taught them *(Lk. 10:38-42)*. He interpreted the times with people *(Lk. 12:54-56)*. While traveling along he healed a blind beggar *(Lk. 18:35-43)*. The point is, Jesus served where opportunity presented itself. He often taught under the same circumstances *(cf. Lk. 22:24-30)*.

The common ministry of reconciliation given to all disciples is often unfulfilled for lack of grasping the opportunities at hand.

Chapter II

IF THE CHURCH IS ALL THAT, WHERE IS THE BEEF?

The Christian Church as the body of Christ is a beautiful and noble ideal. It is perfection personified. It takes its beauty and nobility from Christ. The image of the invisible God is the head of the body, the Church. From him the body receives its character. As the ideal community, the Church is also a goal to be achieved by the institutional Church. The institutional Church is the visible body of Christ populated by imperfect human beings. On the one hand its members participate in perfection; and on the other hand, they embody imperfection. I believe that experience supports the position that the Church is both being and becoming. And we, Pulpit and Pew, pastor and people share in both.

The beef, then, is in the reality that the Church we see, the visible institution where we hold membership or serve as pastor is imperfect. The Church has always been that way. Its population in every place is sinful. They sin and do things that are less than good or perfect. Many manifestations of their sinfulness are revealed. Let us consider a few of them. Let us consider reasons why the unity and harmony of the body of Christ is disturbed.

One, some members have only a shallow commitment to the common good. The interest and well-being of the body is less important than the desire and pleasure of some members. When the shameful behavior of some members of the Church at Corinth is analyzed, it is revealed that they were insensitive to the importance of some other members to the well-being of the body. In the celebration of Holy Communion, it appears that the well-to-do members did not wait for the poorer members to get off work and get to the meeting.

The behavior at the Lord's Supper only expressed what was wrong among these who supped. Paul put his finger on the problem with the words, "to begin with, when you come together as a church, I hear there are divisions among you..." *(I Cor. 11:18)*. The problem Paul pointed to symbolizes the background of many causes for disharmony in churches. Individuals bring unresolved situations with them to worship, to Prayer Meeting and Bible Study, and to Church business meetings. As the divisions within the Church at Corinth played themselves out at the time to eat, "each of you goes ahead with your own supper, and one goes hungry and another becomes drunk" *(I Cor. 11:21)*, individual problems as well as group problems manifest themselves in meetings of Church organizations, choir rehearsals and business meetings.

To some extent and in some ways at the celebration of the Lord's Supper the unity and oneness of the Church is always at risk. By their divisiveness, members of the Church at Corinth violated the very nature of the Church. Christ's body is symbolized in the one bread and the one cup a divided Church that partakes of the one bread and the one cup without examining themselves, "drink judgment against themselves" *(I Cor. 11:28, 29)*. The risk of violating the unity of Christ is lessened when members today take seriously the words of invitation, "Ye that do truly and earnestly repent of your sins and are in love and charity with your neighbor, and intend to lead a new life." Repentance indicates a change of mind and a change of direction. It suggests that whatever threatens to divide the body of Christ no longer has a hold on one's heart and mind. The intention is to go in a new direction, leading a

new life, "following the commandments of Almighty God."
When that is the set of the mind and the desire of the heart
and the motivation of the will, the common good again
takes center stage.

Two, Church members have divided loyalties. Their
allegiances are of such that God in Christ is not central.
Loyalties to individuals in congregations remove God as the
center of the lives of members. God's command, "you
shall have no other gods before me," is either not honored,
or it is contaminated with a foreign spirit. Again, it was
the Church at Corinth that evidenced divided loyalties.
Individual members of the Church said of themselves, "I
belong to Paul." He was founder of the Church at Corinth.
Certain members of churches cling to the organizing
pastor, or to the pastor who was serving when a church
building was built, or to the mortgage-payer pastor.
Charter members may also claim special privileges. Others
said, "I belong to Apollos." The eloquent Apollos who
was mighty in the Scriptures *(Acts 18:24)*, served the Church
at Corinth *(Acts 19:1)*. His preaching probably made quite an
impression there. Attachments often result from preaching

gifts of pastors. Some members take pride in showing off to others their preaching pastor.

Still others said, "I belong to Cephas ..." Cephas was recognized as a leader of the Church. Three years after Paul's Damascus Road experience he went up to Jerusalem to see Peter, with whom he remained fifteen days *(Gal. 1:18)*. I believe Paul's trip to Jerusalem "to visit Cephas," ... "But I did not see any other apostles except James the Lord's brother" *(19)*, is indicative of Cephas' standing. He was as we know the first apostle put into missions involving Gentiles. Paul's ministry to Gentiles gave him a special need to be conversant with Cephas.

Cephas' position of prominence made him attractive to some members. Association with individuals of power and prominence is attractive to some Church members. Cephas fit that category. And so do some former pastors today to whom members hold onto.

Finally, some said, "I belong to Christ." This group presented a problem for me for a long time. Until I came upon an interpretation I could accept. The problem stemmed from my feeling that there could be nothing possibly wrong with members saying, "I belong to Christ."

After all, Christ is the one to whom all members should belong. Then I came upon the interpretation that regarded the "I belong to Christ" members as the ultra self righteous. Behavior resulting from that attitude can be divisive and disruptive.

Unfortunately, today, there is a re-emergence of the use of self-righteous language in services of public worship. Pastors make "religion" a matter of verbal behavior, such as saying, "Amen," or "Hallelujah" or by using formulae such as, "God is good," followed by the response, "All the time." Or, "All the time," followed by "God is good." Only those who participate in the ritual meet and pass the test!

Another divide between those who "got something" *(Religion?)* and those who "ain't got nothing" *(No religion?)* is through physical actions, such as hand waving, or, lifting holy hands, or giving God a hand clap or hand praise, or some love.

In this context, Paul raised a tongue-in-cheek question. "Has Christ been divided?" *(I Cor. 1:13).* Of course not. But there are those who think themselves the only real and true Christians.

Three, pastor-envy on the part of members. It may seem to some that the illustration used here is stretched to make the point. Nonetheless, the point is important and relevant for describing current situations. Though the illustration be strained, if the point remains intact that is the important thing. Indeed, friction rises in congregations where individuals take on their pastor. I have called it pastor-envy. Miriam and Aaron had a problem with Moses. It is more correct to say that Miriam had a problem. Numbers 12:1 includes both in the words, "While they were at Hazeroth, Miriam and Aaron spoke against Moses because of the Cushite *(Ethiopian)* woman whom he had married ..." However, only Miriam was inflicted with leprosy. It is quite true that the Lord included both in his denunciation.

I take my cue not from Moses' marriage to an Ethiopian woman but from the words, "Has the Lord spoken only through Moses? Has he not spoken through us also?" Clearly these are words of jealousy and envy. After all, Miriam was a prophetess *(Exod. 15:20)*. She did not want to accede to Moses' special position before God. Which is a denial of some church members regarding their pastors. A thesis of this author is that the Pulpit or pastor has a special place in God's Church. It is true that "God has a few into whose ears He whispers." King Zedekiah must have known that. When Judah was faced with certain defeat at the hands of the Chaldeans King Zedekiah sent for Jeremiah. When Jeremiah arrived, the King asked, "Is there any word from the Lord?" *(Jer. 37:17)*.

The specially chosen of God are protected by God. He said, "Do not touch my anointed ones; do my prophets no harm" *(I Chron. 16:22)*. When persons deny a special place to the Pulpit or pastor, the ground is removed for not touching nor harming them. They are reduced to the masses. However, I am persuaded that God has always elected individuals from among the multitudes for special or peculiar roles and functions. In our illustration story, God called Moses for a special role. That role put him out front. So it is with the pastor. Being gifted by Christ to be pastor and teacher *(Eph. 4:11)*, the pastor is placed out front.

God's anger came through against Miriam and Aaron and He called them with Moses "to the tent of meeting" *(Numb. 12:4)*. He said,

Hear my words: When there are prophets among you, I the Lord make myself known to them in visions; I speak to them in dreams.

Not so with my servant Moses; he is entrusted with all my house.

With him I speak face to face--clearly, not in riddles; and he beholds the form of the Lord.

Why then were you not afraid to speak against my servant Moses?

Numb. 12:6-8

For individuals who demonstrate, for whatever reasons, pastor-envy, two things are said. Pastor or Pulpit has a special place based on function, but that place is not exempt from divine judgment. Recall what I wrote in Chapter One on shepherds. Every disciple of Christ is accountable for how well they do the job to which God calls them. Jesus' parable of the talents illustrates that accountability. The mai in the parable who entrusted his property to his slaves before going away on a journey may be likened to Christ. He gave one slave five talents, to another two and to a third he gave one. The slaves with five and two talents told the Master upon his return they had doubled their trusts. The slave who had received one talent buried his and when the Master returned attempted to justify his behavior by appealing to the harsh character of the Master. Judgment fell heavy on this "wicked and lazy slave" *(Matt. 25:14-30)*.

Second, instead of Pew or people attacking the Pulpit or pastor and instead of refusing to hear the Word delivered by them, energy, effort and commitment must be dedicated to investing their talents.

Pew or people have received gifts by the spirit. In the interest of unity and ministry members enhance these when they understand the nature of the Church as the body of Christ. "For as in one body we have many members, and not all the members have the same function" *(Rom. 12:4)*, all members contribute to body harmony by affirming "not all the members have the same function." Members "have gifts that differ" and they do so not based on human ability and capacity, but "according to the grace given to us" *(Rom. 12:6)*.

All "gifts" are given by grace. Whether your gift is singing, or preaching, or ushering, or administration, or cooking, or driving, or leading, or mediating, your gift is

God's gift to you.   Your thing is "not to think of yourself more highly than you ought to think" *(Rom. 12:3)*.   All must "think with sober judgment."   For the several gifts with different functions were given for "the common good."   As such they all are necessary.   Each member must "think soberly."   On the one hand, each member, Pulpit and Pew, must know his or herself as well as each knows her or his place.   No one can do everything.   Sober thinking reveals as much.   No one should deny others their places.   The good of the whole is served by sober judgment.   After all God has assigned a "measure of faith" to everyone.   This faith is "the regulative standard."   If we "think soberly" about our particular God-given gift, we know our limitation.   An individual's voice, whether used for singing or preaching, has limitations.   One person's voice can achieve things another cannot.   The same is true in the case of other gifts.   God has assigned a measure of faith to each, sober thinking lets us know and accept without regret or envy of others our limitations.   More importantly, we must not understand limitations to mean inferior.   Instead, limitations mean God has not given to anyone of us every gift.   He distributes the gifts.   Should He give all of the gifts to any one in a congregation God would, more likely than not, increase the possibility of confusion. That one person might become "too big." With the gifts distributed, Pulpit has a place of prominence. Members may give honor and preference to Pulpit. But before you are envious, reflect on how Pulpit's high profile position makes him or her a fit target of attack. Are you envious of that?

Four, some members, Pulpit and Pew, by hypocritical behavior, create disharmony. Hypocrisy is a matter of wearing two different faces. Where unity in Christ is essential and that is the case in the body of Christ, one individual wearing different faces creates confusion. Christ is not divided so there is consistency in truth and behavior. If it is truth today, it was so yesterday, and will be tomorrow. The same may be said about right Christian behavior. Essentials do not change from day to day. Stability is dependent upon consistency. Where uncertainty exists as to truth and behavior community life is virtually impossible. Around these discipline may be structured.

Peter and Paul had a face-to-face showdown in Antioch. The issue was Peter's inconsistent behavior relative to eating with Gentiles *(Gal. 2:1-14)*. Peter had supposedly lost his bias against this eating after he had a vision in Joppa on the roof of Simon the tanner's house. By his own admission to Cornelius, his relatives and friends in Caesarea, he said, "God has shown me that I should not call anyone profane or unclean" *(Acts 10:28)*. He reported his experience to the Church in Jerusalem, how, while he was speaking Cornelius and the other Gentiles with him had the Holy Spirit fall upon them, "As it had upon us at the beginning" *(Acts 11:15)*. The church was silenced by what they heard. "And they praised God, saying, "Then God has given even to the Gentiles the repentance that leads to life" *(18)*.

Paul charged Peter with following what he claimed to have been shown and told by God was right, only under certain circumstances. Before certain people came from James, Paul said of Peter, "he used to eat with the Gentiles. But, after they came, he drew back and kept himself separate for fear of the circumcision faction" *(Gal. 2:12)*. Peter's own inconsistent behavior relative to revealed truth was bad enough on its own. But it had a wider influence. That is always the case regardless of the nature of the action. Paul said, "the other Jews joined him in this hypocrisy, so that even Barnabas was led astray by their hypocrisy." *(13)*.

Where inconsistency in truth is normative in a congregation, members have no standard on which to develop their belief system and their teaching. Inconsistency in what is true leads to wavering behavior. Ethics is religion based. Without a stable base of truth, behavior is without a foundation. Where truth changes, proper, correct and right things to do become cloudy.

Blessed is a congregation of saints of God in Christ of whom it may be said, "Remember your leaders, those who spoke the word of God to you; consider the outcome of their way of life, and imitate their faith. Jesus Christ is the same yesterday and today and forever. Do not be carried away with all kinds of strange teaching" *(Heb. 13:7-9a)*. A congregation with leaders, Pulpit and Pew, who strive to avoid hypocritical speech and actions, ever standing in the teaching of the unchanging Jesus, is fortunate. The members have precepts and examples to follow.

Five, selfish self-interests threaten the interest of the whole. The large wheel of a wagon is a visible image of how the Church may regard itself. The hub in the middle to which the spokes are anchored from their outer limits provides a symbol of Christ into whom all Church members have been initiated. Each member is important to maintaining a firm outer presence in the world, whose unity is symbolized by the outer rim. When a spoke or spokes become loose within the hub, they sometime slip from the hold in the outer rim. After a time, the whole design begins to lose its shape, firmness and ability to do its job, which is to bear weight and roll, or move. A loosely connected Church body will lose its ability to do its job, worship, fellowship and serve.

A threat to a Church remaining healthy enough to do its job is individual members turning away from concern and interest in the common good to "my good." Luke provides a discussion that illustrates the point. The words, "A dispute also arose among them as to which one of them was to be regarded as the greatest" *(22:24)*. Now this is not the only time a dispute had arisen among them on the question of greatness. A common thread between Luke 22:24-30 and Luke 9:46-48 is when each happened. Each occasion of the "argument" *(9:46)* or "dispute" *(22:24)*, is after Jesus' death had been a matter of teaching, directly or indirectly. Not only did the disciples' implied question of greatness reflect insensitivity to Jesus' situation, it diverted attention away from what was very important, group unity rather than individual status.

I will connect this discussion with another event in the life of Jesus' disciples. My point in doing so is to suggest that disputing and arguing about greatness had a negative effect on the job they had been called to do. Engagement in arguments and other extraneous matters by Church members, Pulpit and Pew, pastor and people, divert from growing in faith which enables them to be effective disciples of Christ.

The connecting story has to do with the inability of eight of Jesus' disciples to cast a demon out of a boy whose father had requested them to do it *(cf. Matt. 17:14-21)*. The other three disciples, Peter, James, and John, had gone with Jesus "up a high mountain," where "he was transfigured before them" *(Matt. 17:1-8)*. All twelve of them had received "authority to cast out demons" *(Mk. 3:15)*. But when the nine tried to exercise the authority to cast the demon out of the boy "they could not" *(Matt. 17:16)*.

Why could the disciples not cast out the demon? Jesus said it was, "Because of your little faith" *(20)*. It is obvious from Jesus' later use of a mustard seed to describe faith that quality of faith and not quantity was their problem. The disciples had not done the things necessary for their faith to grow. Apparently their observation of Jesus and the works he did, nor his teaching had adequately impacted their faith. Instead, the focus of their concern was themselves and their future greatness. Matthew's account reveals the negative fallout from James and John's mother asking Jesus to, "Declare that these two sons of mine will sit, one at your right hand and one at your left, in your kingdom." When Jesus told them, "You do not know what you are asking. Are you able to drink the cup that I am about to drink?" they said, "We are able." And Matthew wrote: "When the ten heard it, they were angry with the two brothers." Jesus called all twelve of the disciples to him and taught that true greatness comes through service and not through the ruthless exercise of authority *(cf. Matt. 20:20-28)*.

Jesus called all of his disciples to himself and taught them for in all of them lurked the potentially disruptive desire to be great *(cf. Lk. 9:46-48)*. Could it be that the disciples were impressed more with the way, "the rulers of the Gentiles lord it over, and their great ones are tyrants over them" *(Matt. 20:25)*, than they were by Jesus' teaching, where he used a little child to illustrate greatness *(Matt. 18:1-5)*?

Where Pulpit and Pew focus on self and its selfish desires the harmony of the fellowship is at risk.

Six, a pastor suffering burn-out is a drag on his or her effectiveness and on the well-being of the congregation. Burn out is a total condition of a human being. It results often from over-work. And reflects itself in a depletion that is mental, physical and spiritual. Efforts made to fulfill one's duties at work, in the home, church, or community are little more than wheel spinning. Tempers are short. Human faculties especially thinking and acting are sluggish. It is not uncommon for the burnt out to feel as did the psalmist when he asked, "Why are you cast down, O my soul, and why are you disquieted within me?" *(Ps. 42:5)*

Total fatigue renders Pulpit incapable of functioning to the level of his or her abilities. As suggested above, tired minds and tired bodies make for a devastating combination. They create individuals who will not accept the fact of their condition and attempting to go on they are burdensome to all they work with and live with.

The story of Jethro and Moses *(Exod. 18)*, provides insights into a possible cause for burn-out and preventive medicine. Essentially it is a story of leadership or the lack of it. Jethro visited Moses, his son-in-law, and soon discovered that he was doing all the work of judging the people, doing it all by himself. From morning until evening the people stood around Moses to inquire of God and to have him settle disputes between two disputing individuals. Jethro's words to Moses reveal that what Moses was doing would affect him and the people. He said, "What you are doing is not good. You will surely wear yourself out, both you and these people with you. For this task is too heavy for you; you cannot do it alone" *(Exod. 18:17-18)*.

Jethro noted that Moses had a one-man show. He did it all, everything. Pulpit or pastor may not only do everything, but may really believe the only way for it to get done right is to do it himself or herself. Pew, or the people, are left standing around doing nothing. Frequently while watching basketball on television, a team that is ahead on points will begin to lose the lead. The game announcer often states that the problem is while one player has the ball dribbling it, the other players just stand around. They are not moving, thus, they are out of the flow of the action. One man, not five, was all of the action. That approach causes games to be lost.

Jethro wisely suggested a better way to Moses. He offered him *a shared leadership style.* One that involved other leaders. Pulpit or pastor that would not become too quickly burnt out should assess his or her leadership style. Is yours a one-person show? Do you do everything yourself? Or, do you delegate responsibility? Having done so, do you use your gift of administration to equip those to whom you delegate responsibility?

Jethro's proposal to Moses placed him where pastor or shepherd to God's flock ought to be. A great deal of teaching on the doctrine of the "priesthood of believers" has taken the unique place of the pastor out of the economy of God. I want to put it back and it can be done without violating the right and privilege of the Pew to go boldly to the throne of grace. The directive in Jethro's proposal is of the same spirit of my position. He told Moses the first piece of his proposal is: "Stand before God for the people." That to me is the pastor's role. I experience too many pastors who do not offer the pastoral prayer in Sunday worship service. They do not stand "before God for the people." A shepherd who knows his or her sheep, who sits where they sit all week, should, on the Sabbath, stand before God for them. Their joys and sorrows, their defeats and victories, their ups and downs, the pastor should carry to the Lord in prayer.

Jethro indicated that Moses should not leave the people without some responsibility for themselves. He was to "bring the difficulties to God." The rulers would deal with the lesser matters. It may be said that church officers should handle matters that they are able to handle. Thereby, the Pastor should take care of difficult matters.

Moses, like a good pastor, was not to be turned towards God and away from the people always. In fact Moses was not only to speak to God, he was to listen, also. That is what prayer is. It is communion with God, which is both listening and speaking. What Moses received from

God was to be taught to the people in "statutes and laws."
Through the teaching, Moses was to "show them the way
in which they must walk and the work they must do" *(20)*.
Pulpit does this through preaching and teaching. After
meditating, the pastor proclaims a God-inspired message to
God's people in waiting.

Jethro instructed Moses to select able, truthful,
hating covetousness, God-fearing men and place them as
rulers over groups of thousands, rulers of hundreds, rulers
of fifties, and rulers of ten *(21, NKJV)*. These rulers were to
judge the people at all times. Only great matters would be
brought to Moses. Pulpit or pastor should not be called
upon to referee every Church fight, or to put out every
brush fire. Officers selected by the pastors ought to be
trained or equipped to take care of "every small matter"
(22).

Jethro's final words to Moses on this matter assured
him that if he did "this thing, and God so commands you,
then you will be able to endure, and all this people will go
to their place in peace" *(23 NKJV)*. Peace among God's
people, already given by Jesus' death on the cross *(Eph.
2:14-18)*, is what God wills for His Church. A pastor who

guards his or her physical health is in a better position, for doing so, to contribute to that peace. Also, Pew who rests from time to time thinks better for it, is easier to be around and to get along with. In retrospect, I can say to Pulpit, you owe it to your family to take care of your body as well as your soul. Family members worry about pastors who work themselves into bad health and bad dispositions. And congregations suffer when Pulpit is burnt out.

Seven, when good people fail to provide leadership in a Church, it will fall into the hands of those without God's Spirit. The late Bishop J. Claude Allen of the Christian Methodist Episcopal Church used to say that if an appointed pastor does not pastor the congregation it would not be long without a pastor. For there are always "pastors" on site waiting to pastor. What he was saying was that where a vacuum exists in leadership, it will be filled. A leadership vacuum draws and pulls available persons to fill it.

Pulpit and Pew have the responsibility for using their God-given gifts in the Church. Failure to exercise gifts of leadership creates a dangerous vacuum. With a vacuum existing, leadership may fall into the wrong hands.

I share with you Jotham's fable in Judges 9:8-15. It is a fable about talking trees. You remember, it was Jotham the youngest of the seventy sons of Jerubbaal who was the only survivor of the group slaughtered by "worthless and reckless fellows" whom Abimelech hired to kill all seventy. With sixty nine of the sons of Jerubbaal dead, Abimelech was made king.

Jotham climbed to the top of Mount Gerizim and spoke his fable of the trees. He said the trees once went forth to anoint a king over them. They said to the olive tree, "Come reign over us." The olive tree offered its excuse and refused.

Next, they said to the fig tree, "Come you, and reign over us." Again they were refused. Then, the trees approached the vine and said, "Come you, and reign over us." The vine refused their invitation, also.

Finally, all the trees said to the bramble, "Come you, and reign over us." The bramble took up the offer of the trees. He said, "If in good faith you are anointing me king over you, then come and take refuge in my shade; but if not, let fire come out of the bramble and devour the cedars of Lebanon" *(15)*.

The best qualified refused and one without qualifications took leadership. The bramble knows he is unsuitable. He is a last resort. He knows he cannot hold sway over the other trees. His shade is sparse and if they sit they will be prostrate and pricked. He has power to harm them. But this is what churches end up with when good people are too busy to help out. They end up with unqualified, unspiritual, sometime mean leadership.

Eight, declared "hell raisers" are a menace to the unity and growth of the Church. I suppose every congregation has its antagonists. Sometime they take their role seriously and regard their antagonistic ways as principled. They do what they do from principle. Others may disagree with their principles but to them, they are sound.

Paul referred to some of the people in Philippi as "the dogs" and "the evil workers." Those are good names for "hell raising members." Paul warned the Church at Philippi saying, "Beware of the dogs; be on your guard against the evil workers." In the Bible, the dog is not "man's best friend." To the contrary, nothing is lower than a dog *(cf. I Sam. 24:14; II Kings 8:13).* In the parable of the Rich Man and Lazarus, part of the torture of Lazarus is that the street dogs annoy him by licking his sores *(Lk. 16:20)*. In Deuteronomy the Law brings together the price of a dog and the hire of a whore, and declares that neither must be offered to God *(Deut. 23:18)*. In Revelation, the word dog stands for those who are so impure that they are debarred from the Holy City *(Rev. 22:15)*.[5]

"Evil workers" are individuals who do evil things. Dogs and evil workers have names. They are not "Anonymous." You will know them by their works. Paul named Alexander, the coppersmith, as one I call a "Hell raiser." Paul said, "He did me great harm."

Should Pew name the hell raisers in a congregation? Paul told Timothy that Alexander had done him much harm. But notice that Paul made the object of Alexander's opposition more significant than himself. Alexander resisted "our words," or, "our message" *(II Tim. 4:14-15)*. Anyone who opposes the Gospel qualifies for the "dog" label. Members who are without Christ in their lives have no scruples. They are capable of all types of ungodly

---

[5]*Daily Study Bible Series, The Gospel of Luke*, p. 54.

behavior. Christ provides constraints to be placed upon their behavior. Where the words of the Gospel are resisted the Pew may do the pulpit great harm. It is virtually impossible to reason with "hell raisers" who refuse to hear God's Word. Which leads me to say churches may have to put such members out of their fellowship. While there is debate on whether members ought to be put out or not, putting them out for cause is biblically supported *(Matt. 18:15-20)*. For a different approach, read Second Timothy 2:20-26.

    Nine, Pulpit or pastor may have entered the ministry for the wrong reason and will stop at nothing to gain power and prestige. The call to preach is a personal affair. Samuel's call was shared with Eli but no one else heard the voice that called out, saying, "Samuel, Samuel" *(I Sam. 3:10)*.

    Isaiah alone experienced the Lord in the temple. He was the one who was asked, "Whom shall I send, and who will go for us?" *(Isa. 6:8 KJV)*

    When Jesus was called after his baptism by John the Baptist, he was the one who heard a voice from heaven, saying, "This is My beloved Son, in whom I am well pleased" *(Matt. 3:17 KJV)*. Even Saul of Tarsus surrounded by other men was the only one who knew that he encountered Jesus on the Damascus Road. He was the only one addressed by the voice that asked, "Saul, Saul, why are you persecuting Me?" Having been addressed, Saul asked, "Who are you, Lord?" The persecutor acknowledged the fact that he met his match. He called the Speaker "Lord." The one who had arrested Saul of Tarsus said, "I am Jesus, ..." *(Acts 9:4-5, NKJV)*

The fact that the call to preach and to pastor is personal, even private, means it has its own set of difficulties. Arrogance is not an uncommon partner of the call. Preachers bristle and challenge any and all who dare question the authenticity of their call. They feel at one with Paul who said to the Church at Galatia:

> *For I want you to know, brothers and sisters, that the gospel that was proclaimed by me is not of human origin; for I did not receive it from a human source, nor was I taught it, but I received it through a revelation of Jesus Christ.*
> Gal. 1:11-12

Paul boldly claimed a direct line to Christ. You recall his words regarding the Lord's Supper.

> *For I received from the Lord what I also*
> *handed on to you, that the Lord Jesus on the*
> *night when he was betrayed took a loaf of*
> *bread, and when he had given thanks, he*
> *broke it and said, "This is my body that is*
> *for you. Do this in remembrance of me."*
> *In the same way he took the cup also, after*
> *supper, saying, "This cup is the new*
> *covenant in my blood. Do this, as often as*
> *you drink it, in remembrance of me." For*
> *as often as you eat this bread and drink the*
> *cup, you proclaim the Lord's death until he*
> *comes.*
> I Cor. 11:23-26

I refuse to pass judgment on any claim whether it be the personal-private nature of the call to preach or the claim of a direct line to God in sermon preparation without use of outside resources. But I will say Paul's works spoke for him *(cf. II Cor. 3:1-2)*.

The personal-private nature of the call to preach allows anyone to enter the ministry. I am aware that John Wesley held and so does the Christian Methodist Episcopal Church that the truly called ought to show some fruits from their preaching. However, experience shows that the committed and the charlatan may have the same results from their labors. I share with you the story of one, Simon.

Simon lived in the city of Samaria. He was a sorcerer or the worker of magic. Philip went to Samaria and was received very well. As the late Bishop P. Randolph Shy of the Christian Methodist Episcopal Church used to say after one preached, "He was heard to great advantage today," which was a high compliment.

Simon was greatly acclaimed. Luke said, "All of them, from the least to the greatest listened to him eagerly, saying, "This man is the power of God that is called Great" *(Acts 8:10)*. Simon, some scholars maintain, laid claim to deity and actually seized upon the expectation of Messiah using it to his advantage. Some in the pulpit, today, manipulate people by exploiting their longings and their frustrations. Unfortunately, many people are easy prey for anyone who comes claiming to come in the name of the Lord. They give and send them money, sometime contributing more to tele-evangelists and to some traveling hucksters than they contribute to the local church where they hold membership.

Philip was a great hit in Samaria, the people believed the Gospel he preached and were baptized. Simon himself believed and was baptized. Afterwards he remained with Philip. Word reached Jerusalem that Samaria had accepted the word of God. So Peter and John were sent and they came and prayed for the believers that they might receive the Holy Spirit. Also, they laid hands on them and they received the Holy Spirit.

Now, it is interesting that Simon, who believed and was baptized, was not among those who received the Holy Spirit through the imposition of the apostles' hands. Why? Had he negatively impressed them so they excluded him? We are not told. We are told that after Simon saw that the Holy Spirit was given through the laying on of hands, he offered to pay for it. He said, "Give me also this power so that anyone on whom I lay my hands shall receive the Holy Spirit" *(19)*.

This man who had amazed people with his magic thought if he could lay on hands and impart the Holy Spirit he would be an even bigger hit. It is a travesty upon grace for anyone to try to buy the power of the Holy Spirit to use for ego gratification and selfish monetary gain. Likewise, it would have been a sin and shame had Peter sold power for money. Of course he could not do so. The Holy Spirit is God's to give, the apostles' hands were mere means.

Ten, the refusal of Pulpit and Pew, pastor and people to fulfill the vow of church membership is a cancerous disease eating at the heart and soul of the church's unity and harmony.

Every member of the Christian Methodist Episcopal Church and I suppose all denominations are required to make a commitment or promise or vow of Church membership. The Christian Methodist Episcopal Church's vow of membership asks a six-fold promise. It asks, "Will you be subject to the Discipline of the Christian Methodist Episcopal Church? and be loyal to it? and you will uphold the Christian Methodist Episcopal Church by your prayers, your presence, your gifts and your service?"

The well-being of the Church is maintained by members, clergy and lay, Pulpit and Pew, faithfulness to that vow. Pulpit or pastor may take other vows later, but that basic vow remains critical. Beneath the individual promises in the vow is a profound spiritual element. It is like a fabric that is held together by the individual faithfulness of all who make it. The Church as the creation of the Spirit is held together by spiritual things and by spiritual relationships. Nothing is more important on the human side than human dependability, which requires the ability to trust one another. That ability it either helped or hindered by how every member keeps his or her word. When the word is not kept, the fabric is damaged. For every member is part of every other member. Each has a part to play. Moreover, unfaithfulness by one damages the whole. There is a mystery, if you will, in things that are truly spiritual. Paul said this about the unity in the Spirit: "If one member suffers, all suffer together with it; if one member is honored, all rejoice together with it" *(I Cor. 12:26)*. When a member or members fail to keep the vow and covenant of Church membership all members suffer, just as all are strengthened by the faithfulness of any or all.

Ananias and Sapphira were "members" of the apostolic church *(Acts 5:1-11)*. With all others they voluntarily vowed to hold in common everything they owned. "There was not a needy person among them for as many as owned lands or houses sold them and brought the proceeds of what was sold. They laid it at the apostles' feet, and it was distributed to each as any had need" *(Acts 4:34-35)*. It is small wonder why Luke described their unity with the words, "Now the whole group of those who believed were of one heart and soul, ..." *(Acts 4:3)*.

Ananias and Sapphira who were part of this covenant sold land but by mutual agreement held back a portion of the proceeds. They failed to keep their word. Peter's chastisement of them includes a statement that fingers the true nature of unfaithfulness to the religious vow. He said, "You did not lie to us but to God" *(5:4d)*. Often church members, Pulpit and Pew, fail to understand the human-divine relationship in the vow made. The pastor before whom we stand and take a vow of membership is only a stand in for Christ. That is awesome, yet true. We may know them so well until we feel about them as the people in Nazareth felt about Jesus *(Matt. 13:54-58)*. Their knowledge of Jesus was correct but incomplete. It was what was lacking in their knowledge that was critical. Jesus' divinity, or his Sonship, if you will, was not acceptable. The people could not grasp that this man from Nazareth was God's Christ.

Ananias and Sapphira were judged harshly for lying to God. They died. Their deaths were physical. Hopefully, ours will not reach that extreme. But our judgment will be severe indeed. Violation of vows of Church membership brings death to the spirit. All who die spiritually are the walking dead. Unlike Ananias and Sapphira who "fell down and died," we who violate our vows of Church membership stand and walk dead.

This death is a matter of a rejected conscience. Conscience keeps us sensitive to good and evil, right and wrong. Failure to keep promises made to God lead eventually to a loss of conscience. After awhile it no longer bothers us, nor matters. The inner spirit dies. Paul wrote to Timothy about keeping a good conscience and what happened to some who lost their's.

> *I am giving you these instructions, Timothy, my child, in accordance with the prophecies made earlier about you, so that by following them you may fight the good fight, having faith and a good conscience. By rejecting conscience, certain persons have suffered shipwreck in the faith; among them are Hymenaeus and Alexander, whom I have turned over to Satan, so that they may learn not to blaspheme.*

I Tim. 1:18-20

Notice the words "suffered shipwreck in the faith," which are Paul's description of what happened to some Church members including Hymenaeus and Alexander who were guilty of "rejecting conscience."

The vow of Church membership is to be kept in all of its aspects. One aspect is no greater than any other. If they were promised for conscience sake and the well-being of the Church, keep them.

Eleven, where a member who knows the right thing to say, then, but keeps silent, contributes to the decline and deterioration of unity and stability. As a local Church pastor, I experienced the same thing I have had scores of pastors tell me as a Bishop that they experienced, too. Generically, the experience begins in an official business meeting of the congregation. Pulpit or pastor presides in the meeting. An issue comes up on the agenda in which pastor has modest interest in its passage. Once that interest is revealed, Alexander the coppersmith makes a personal attack on pastor *(II Tim. 4:14)*. No one rises to say a word in defense of pastor. Every pastor with an experience of that type possibly knows how Paul felt when he told

Timothy, "At my first defense no one came to my support, but all deserted me" *(II Tim. 4:16)*.

The story continues! After the meeting is over, invariably, a well meaning, yet spineless, member, comes up beside pastor outside of the meeting room and says, "Pastor, I'm with you." A few minutes earlier pastor felt secure for one reason only. Which Paul stated also to Timothy, "But the Lord stood by me and gave me strength ..." *(II Tim. 4:17)*.

Experiences such as the one being discussed, when perpetrators of attacks on pastor go unchallenged, tend to be divisive. Underneath the silence of good yet timid members, is support for pastor, who I am assuming is in the right. On the other hand, the silence of other members who support the attacker indicate a broader base of opposition than verbal involvement would suggest. When the two positions are evaluated, they equal divisions. Which existed already and were revealed or made known by the issue raised.

Would another member speaking up have changed anything? Naturally, pre-existing divisions were not created by what happened. Nonetheless, a voice of reason may have caused both sides to wait before taking action on the matter. It is surprising what impact and influence waiting can have on what appeared urgent. Crucial to the outcome are factors such as the respectability of the one who takes up the cause, the approach used, and the rationale for the approach suggested.

I return again and again to Gamaliel the grandson of the renowned Hillel, the most influential teacher of the Pharisees. Gamaliel was a doctor, or authoritative teacher, of the Law. This man impresses me with the way he handled a potentially violent situation in the Sanhedrin Council of which he was a member. The apostles were before the council for the second time in short order. These men simply refused to stop proclaiming the Gospel even under threat by the Sanhedrin. The second time around the council "was engaged and wanted to kill them" *(Acts 5:33)*.

Gamaliel took charge. He was highly respected. He was calm in his approach, calling for reason. He reminded them of others, Theudas and Judas the Galilean, who rose up claiming to be somebody. Both of them failed in their pursuits. So what should they do? They should, "keep away from these men and let them alone" *(38a)*. Why should this powerful body of men back off from twelve virtual nobodies? Gamaliel reasoned, thus; "if this plan or this undertaking is of human origin, it will fail; but if it is of God, you will not be able to overthrow them--in that case you may even be found fighting against God!" *(Acts 5:38-39)*.

Gamaliel's reasoning may not always hold true especially from the human side. From an ultimate point of view Gamaliel is right. God's dealings even through human beings are always eternal. They are final or ultimate. Within time, these eternal things may be referred to as right or true. In that sense they cannot be overthrown. They are made of God's nature. The pastor who is challenged if the challenge is to something that is right, a setback is not death. It is only a delay. In God's own time, the plan will prevail. Yet good men and women must dare to "speak the truth in love." Their speaking may avoid the widening of divisions in a congregation.

Chapter III

PREVENTING AND FIXING CONFLICT

The community described in Chapter One, "Pulpit And Pew Have Things In Common" has been shown in Chapter Two, "If The Church Is All That, Where Is The Beef?," to be in conflict. In this chapter, we will consider, "Preventing And Fixing Conflict."

What is conflict?

The word "conflict" suggests confrontation between two human beings or two groups. Such confrontation ranges from a lovers' tiff to the threat of nuclear war, and surely the living Gospel has something to say to us all about this aspect of the Christian life as individuals and as members of Christ's Church. The intense humanity and realism of the Bible reflect our human conflicts in every book from Genesis to Revelations.
This could lead us to ask whether the average sermon today is equally honest about the human condition, or are we too anxious to offer peace of mind and self-esteem without reckoning with the sin that

lurks behind most human conflicts and corrupts even the noblest cause.[6]

Dr. David H. C. Read suggested that "sin ... lurks behind most human conflicts and corrupts even the noblest cause." The evangelist James wrote that, "Those conflicts and disputes among you, where do they come from? do they not come from your cravings that are at war within you?"

Paul's First Letter to the Corinthians questions the maturity of the saints in the Church at Corinth and identified their condition as "still in the flesh." Paul said also, "For as long as there is jealousy and quarreling among you, are you not of the flesh, and behaving according to human inclinations? For when one says, "I belong to Paul," and another, "I belong to Apollos," are you not merely human?" *(I Cor. 3:3-4)*

Strife and factions in a congregation reflect the work, not of the Spirit, but of the human flesh *(cf. Gal. 5:15-26)*. These evidence immaturity in the faith and knowledge of God in Christ. "For God is a God not of disorder but

---

[6]David H.C. Read. "Conflict - From Local to the Cosmic," *The Living Pulpit*, July - Sep. 1994, p. 4.

of peace" *(I Cor. 14:33)*.   Anyone who is in Christ cannot accuse God of being behind the confusion, conflict and dissension they cause or enjoin.   That is not God's way. The dissension God creates has a redemptive or salvific purpose.   "The Gospel underlines the call of Jesus to all his disciples to accept not just the rest and refreshment that he promises, but also the trials and even torments.   One of the hard sayings is surely "Do you think that I have come to bring peace to the earth?   No, I tell you, but rather division?" *(Lk. 12:51)*[7]   One of the effects of the ministry of Jesus will be discord and disruption.   It is the result of the fact, that in one way or another every person eventually answers Pilate's question, "what should I do with Jesus who is called the Messiah?" *(Matt. 27:22)*.   The answers divide up the sides.   That is so because individuals decide for Jesus or against him.

Jesus himself was engaged in a conflict between light and darkness, truth and falsehood, right and wrong. Darkness closed in on Jesus as the evening shade began falling as Calvary drew near.   "Jesus sees this as the

---

[7]Ibid

climax of his conflict. The hour has come for the Son of Man to be glorified" *(John 12:23)*.[8]

Conflict began in Eden over the fruit of the tree of knowledge of good and evil. It has continued. It continues.

> *Conflict is inevitable when humans have freedom; because they each have a will; because they will "seek their own"; because even in pursuit of ideals and in expressing the love of God, their wills will clash. But conflict is also usually destructive because the expressers of freedom lose sight of the goals. It distorts each person's vision of the other. The conflictual person or party loses empathy. For the sake of efficiency in effecting one's will, one may end up being concerned only for the self, and losing dependency upon the God who "sitteth in the heaven and laughs"* (Ps. 2:4) *at human pretensions and power. Worst of all, the person or party in conflict likes to call God down to support her on their side.*[9]

Now that we have made conflict inevitable if for no other reason than we sin because we are sinners saved by

---

[8]Read, op. cit., p. 5

[9]Martin E. Marty. "Conflict and Conflict Resolution," *The Living Pulpit*, Jul.-Sept. 1994, p. 12.

grace, an important question is this: "What do we do about it?"

Martin E. Marty says,

Finally, conflict is to be overcome, not by suppressing differences, stomping on freedom, dishonoring will or refusing to listen to voice. Conflict is used to stimulate the imagination, quicken pulses for adventure and force the persons and parties to take on ideas and tasks so great that they become newly reliant on God. Thus they get glimpses of what the apostle Paul and, we must presume, the Holy Spirit, wants: "that you be united in the same mind and the same purpose" (I Cor. 1:10). *Or at least, as with all things on the earthly side of the heavenly kingdom, always be "in the process of being united" because Christ was and is not divided.*[10]

Another crucial question is this: "How do we do what is necessary to resolve conflict?" I will suggest some means whereby we try to prevent what cannot be prevented and how we resolve it once it exists.

First, we must understand the nature and meaning of the context in which conflict occurs. This knowledge

---

[10]Marty, op. cit., p. 13

helps to know that while conflict is inevitable in a living organism, which the Church is, we see that conflict is almost always disruptive and disuniting. Conflict dissipates energy, time, effort, and other human resources. Where Church members, pastor and people, are unaware that unity is a basic aspect of the Church's nature, they do not see the damage conflict does to the well-being and the witness of the Church. On the well-being side, unity is both the nature of the Church's being and its functioning or its working. The being of the Church is of Christ, but, in that human beings make up his body, which is one, quarreling, bickering, fussing and fighting tear into its God-given unity.

The functioning side of unity cannot be separated from being. That is the case because the Church does according to what it is. Paul said as much when he made it clear to the Corinthian Christians that unity is demonstrated when all of the gifts of the Spirit that are given for the common good are working *(cf. 1 Cor. 12:4-11)*. So unity is not ultimately an abstraction. It is how God ordered the Church by equipping the saints with gifts that differ but when all are working according to the end for which God designed each, the Church operates properly. Think of a watch, every gadget has a job to do, when all of the parts are working according to the maker's plan, the watch does what it was made to do, keep correct time. It demonstrates unity through the quality of the time it keeps. So it is with the Church, "as each part is working properly, promotes the body's growth in building itself up in love" *(Eph. 4:16b)*.

Earlier, I spoke of the Church's witness served by unity. I think we have heard non-Christians and Christians alike refer to the divisions in churches and how conflict in a particular church turns them off. They direct to these situations the proverb Jesus quoted to the people in his hometown of Nazareth. He said, "Doctor, cure yourself" *(Lk. 4:23)*, which means the Church's disunity and broken-ness makes a negative statement inside and outside of itself.

When Jesus told his disciples, "By this everyone will know that you are my disciples, if you have love for one another" *(John 13:35)*, he stated the true essence of unity. For God who is One is love *(I John 4:8)*. And "love is from God" *(I John 4:7)*. So in as much as love is one, all who love are "united in love" *(Col. 2:2)*. The presence of love in the bond of unity witnesses to the world and to the Church. It is not to the Church that the witness is made, but to the unity of God and His Son, Jesus the Christ *(cf. John 17:25-26)*.

While the unity of the Church witnesses to the unity of God, Father, Son, and Holy Spirit, the Church does not save. Salvation is of God and through the Church to which has been entrusted the ministry of proclamation of the good news of God's love. Conflict in the Church draws attention to itself and away from God. Rather than serving as a reflection of God's unity, the Church's broken-ness allows people to see through the mirror to the Church itself. Thus, the purpose of the Church, which is mirroring or reflecting Christ, goes unfulfilled and its role of being the dispenser of the message of reconciliation is forfeited. Worst of all, sinners go unsaved. Segments of the world are left unaware of their reconciliation. And the environment in all of its aspects are left unprotected and uncared for.

I turn now to the divisions in the Church as exist in denominations. I do so not because of their existence but to point to their negative impact and influence upon the Church's witness. So much of what keeps us separated into our various ecclesiastical enclaves is directly related to the body of Christ. Some who read these words may reply attacking my ignorance of the history of the issues, or my lack of appreciation for history and tradition, or my failure or refusal at least to acknowledge the complexity of the issues that separate the churches, or my simplistic understanding and proposal for resolution, or my denial of the emotions and the emotial factors associated with each religious organization or denomination.

Whatever arguments are put forth against the facts in my case, they will stand or fall on their own merits. The body of Christ is fragmented by the denial of admission to the Lord's Table by members of one denomination to another. The Lord's Table is violated when one denomination's members will not receive the bread and the cup consecrated by the Pulpit, or the ordained ministry of some others.

Membership in the body of Christ is controlled presumably by the denominations that decide to accept transferring members from one denomination to another without re-baptism based on modes. If Christ baptizes and the Spirit incorporates the baptized into Christ's body, can it be done twice? Is baptism initiation into the denomination or into Christ's body through a local Church? How many times can the same person be initiated ?

The fundamental issue is neither history nor tradition. It is more than strict literal interpretation of Holy Scriptures, it is first and foremost a matter of violating the unity and oneness of the body of Christ. Jesus prayed the Father to make one his Church, then and afterwards. His reason for praying for one-ness was, "so that the world may believe that you sent me" *(John 17:21)*. The absence of one-ness in the body hinders evangelism. Fragmentation in the body of Christ strikes holes in the integrity of the Church's witness in the world.

Christians, Pulpit and Pew, pastor and people, conscious of the impact conflict has on the Church's unity ought to feel duty bound to not contribute to the widening of the gap and to do what each can to resolve conflict. Remember, "if anyone is disposed to be contentious, we have no such custom *(to be so)*, nor do the churches of God" *(I Cor. 11:16)*. In the matter of who causes conflict in any part of the Church, Paul's words, "Examine yourselves" *(I Cor. 11:28)* apply in every instance. Dialogue between denominations is a necessary first step in overcoming divisions leading to some form of unity. But for the dialogue to be more than "the correct thing to do," respect for one another must exist.

Two, the broken-ness in the body of Christ must be the focus of directed teaching. I speak of teaching both in formal settings designed to pass on facts, information and interpretations, such as Bible Study sessions, Institutes, Seminars, Symposia and the like. I also have in mind teaching from the pulpit in Sunday worship services.

Arguments, quarrels, dissensions, leading to factions and schisms are matters and conditions that need addressing. They do not go away with time. Time may allow scabs to grow over wounds. But time does not heal all wounds. Pulsating beneath the scabs are the conditions, the sickness and the disease, that cause and give rise to conflict.

Directed teaching must seek to diagnose the real cause of a particular troubling situation. A pastor of a particular congregation I am familiar with got off to a very fine beginning on that charge. Several months later complaints began to be sent to the Bishop by some members. In conversation with the Pastor, the Bishop was told that the conflict started after he made some changes in the personnel in the Church office. Members had said earlier that the Pastor was lacking in humility. He expressed arrogance, they maintained, by the way he stood on the steps leading to the pulpit. They demonstrated in the Bishop's presence how the Pastor "rared back." By their admissions, he got on their nerves. Cooperation fell off on the part of many in the Pew.

Pastor and people became estranged one from the other. It is difficult to determine whether the strife was the result of pastoral action, or the result of dislike for the Pastor based on emotions.

A pastor assigned to a church was immediately pulled in by some members in the congregation. I have a saying that says, "When you are assigned to a church, go slow with the members who are the first to eat you up. Beware, for they will be the first to spit you out." In the case of the Pastor being discussed, he found that he had violated another cardinal principle. He had not only allowed himself to be eaten by some members, he fell prey to one family on one side of a two family Church. He had failed to walk in the center, veering neither to the right nor to the left.

Was the Pastor at fault? Or, did he, out of a human desire for acceptance, respond to human kindness and hospitality in a setting where divisions were not expected? Did he, then, become a victim, unwittingly? Or, was he pressured by expectations to be successful, so he grabbed the first thing smoking?

Each time the preacher mounted the pulpit to proclaim the Gospel message, distractions began. One Pew person would lift the Church bulletin up to eye level and sitting right in the second row in front of Pulpit would lip read line by line. At a critical point in the sermon she would stand, lift one finger, and tiptoe her way across the front of the Church to an exit door. Why the behavior? She said, "I just hated to hear the man talk. I can't stand his voice."

Also, she was a seminary student assigned to her first pastoral charge. Her presence for her first Sunday at the new church caused quite a stirring. To a member, the membership decided not to receive the new pastor. Why not? The Pastor was a woman. But why, really? The

Bible says "women should be silent in the churches" *(I Cor. 14:34)*. "I permit no woman to teach or to have authority over a man, she is to keep silent" *(I Tim. 2:12)*.

Without consideration for the context of the Scriptures used, the Pew discriminated against the Pulpit based on gender.

Pulpit's wife went regularly to the business meetings of the Church. One night the climate got hot and heavy as the debate on an issue became intense. It was discussion of an issue presented by the Pastor. So his name came up and he spoke in his own defense. Having heard enough and taking as much as she could take, the Pastor's wife rose and spoke pointedly on behalf of her husband. Her tone was strident and her words accusatory and vengeful. The place became silent. For some members, this was the last straw. They had put up with the charges and counter-charges of the Pastor's wife before. But never had she spoken publicly in such a demeaning and disrespectful way. Their discussions were on the issue and not the Pastor, though his name was mentioned.

Conflict arises sometime when individuals take personally remarks intended to address the issue and not the person. A recurring question and concern is the extent to which a pastor's spouse should become involved in the business affairs of the congregation. And how vocal should a spouse become in defending her or his mate.

A couple blessed with the birth of their first child rejoiced and praised God for the blessing. Within a few weeks they approached their pastor about a time when they could present the child for baptism. Their pastor was in his second year at the Church, during which time no baptisms had been done. Being Methodists, the young couple was not prepared for their pastor's answer to their inquiry. He said, "I don't do infant baptism, because I don't believe in it." Shocked and dismayed, they informed the Pastor that as Methodists they were taught that we use three modes of the one baptism, sprinkling, pouring and immersion. His answer was, "That is true. However, it is not the mode. It is the fact that infants cannot profess belief. And, I believe in believers' baptism, only."

To which they asked, "But, Reverend, what of the faith of the believing community?" He said, "That is irrelevant!"

Disturbed by the outcome, the new parents reported the conversation to the officers of the Church. The couples' concern was whether pastors act ethically when the beliefs and practices they vow to uphold are repudiated later when time comes to be faithful to their promises. Naturally, the incident caused animated discussions and divisions.

The congregation consisted of several generations of members. The old saying, "Like priest like people," was true in many ways. Some of the ways were behavior in corporate worship, community outreach, and church administration. Over a period of time, the various pastors had left their impressions on the membership. A change in pastors brought a change in worship behavior. The change itself was not as divisive as was the comments which separated the "saved" from the "unsaved" based upon who lifted holy hands; or the hands waving in the air; or the shouts of "Hallelujah;" or, the "Amen," antiphonally orchestrated.

Jesus said, "Not everyone who says to me, "Lord, Lord," will enter the kingdom of heaven, but only the one who does the will of my Father in heaven" *(Matt. 7:21)*. His words seem to combine saying and doing. They go beyond seeming and say as much. But doing is not arbitrary. It is related to something particular. That is, "the will of my Father in heaven." The Father's will is the ultimate norm for both what Christians say and do.

The congregation split but unevenly over what the salary compensation of the Pastor should be. Pew felt Pulpit was insensitive to the financial condition of the congregation. Pulpit accused Pew of being un-Christian. Pew asked Pulpit to bear with them since he was new and once things settled down, they would revisit the salary issue. Pastor said people were holding out and he deserved more money than they offered him.

> *Let the elders who rule well be considered worthy of double honor, especially those who labor in preaching and teaching for the scripture says, "You shall not muzzle an ox while it is treading out the grain," and, "The laborer deserves to be paid." Never accept any accusation against an elder except on the evidence of two or three witnesses.*
> I Tim. 5:17-19

Directed or intentional teaching is required to resolve conflict, and to reduce its likelihood of happening.

Directed teaching speaks specifically to the subject matter. In this instance, conflict is shorthand for the subject matter. What approach should be taken?

First, Pulpit must be intentional about defining the context in which conflict occurs. The context in this discussion is the Church. What ought to be defined or described is the behavior that befits the Church. In as much as Christians are new beings in Christ, new behavior is expected from them. Paul wrote to Timothy and said, "I hope to come to you soon, but I am writing these instructions to you so that, if I am delayed you may know how one ought to behave in the household of God, which is the church of the living God, the pillar and the bulwark of the truth" *(I Tim. 3:14-15).*

So, I also suggest that a certain type of behavior is to be lived out in the Church. Since I placed responsibility for the instructions on Pulpit and in as much as some of the examples involve Pulpit as perpetrator of conflict, do not these things insure failure of the undertaking? Only so if, of Pulpit, it cannot be said what Paul told Timothy about himself. Namely, "If you put these instructions before the brothers and sisters, you will be a good servant of Christ

Jesus, nourished on the words of the faith and of the sound teaching which you have followed" *(I Tim. 4:6)*. Pastor may fall short but such does not nullify the call of God. Pastor, like people, "toil and struggle" with the demands of *the faith* and blessed are they who do so *in faith*. Falling short is correctable for those who confess and repent of their sins.

What is the nature of the behavior that is proper in the Church? It is not "behaving according to human inclinations" *(I Cor. 3:3)*. It means, "those who live according to the Spirit set their minds on the things of the Spirit ... To set the mind on the Spirit is life and peace" *(Rom. 8:5b, 6b)*.

What is "the mind" that Paul speaks of? Mind "means" to have understanding, to feel or think, or to direct the mind, to seek or strive for ... the mind is the way the spirit of man uses the brain."[11] "The mind of the Spirit" is indicative of believers who use their brain to pursue the ways of "righteousness." Which means "righteous requirement" fulfilled not by our own abilities,

---

[11]*N.T. Study Bible Romans-Corinthians* (Springfield, MO, The Complete Biblical Library, 1989), p. 123.

might or power, but is fulfilled in one word, even in this, "Thou shalt love thy neighbor as thyself" *(Gal. 5:14 KJV)*.

What motivates the mind in its pursuit of righteousness? The mind's motivation is "the will of God." His will is what is "holy and acceptable to God" *(Rom. 12:1)*. I do not believe that those who are "in Christ" have trouble or difficulty knowing what is "holy and acceptable to God." Regarding self, one is "not to think of yourself more highly than you ought to think" *(Rom. 12:3)*, which is the call to humility, a way of regarding oneself as Christ regarded himself *(Philp. 2:5-11)*.

Regarding our attitude towards others, "in humility regard others as better than yourselves. Let each of you look not to your own interests, but to the interests of others" *(Philp. 2:3b-4)*. When this attitude and this action are put in practice, our behavior in Church takes on a new face. "Do to others as you would have them do to you" *(Lk. 6:31)*. This "Golden Rule" within the Church is a positive. For believers love God first, totally, completely, and second, they love their neighbor as they love themselves.

I have followed here what I call "principled positions" rather than "particularized instruction," because situations differ. Principles may be applied to a broad spectrum of concerns and circumstances. Particularized instructions as I mean them are tailor made for specific circumstances.

Therefore, I have used love as the principle norm of behavior in the body of Christ. Behavior emanating from love is not weak, nor is it non-combative. It is behavior characterized by "speaking the truth in love" *(Eph. 4:15)*. Where truth is at issue, people of faith do battle for it. But they fend for it "in love." When Paul advised Timothy to "Fight the good fight of the faith ..." *(I Tim. 6:12)*, he introduced a side of conflict that is spiritual. The battle in churches involved Pulpit and Pew, and those involved Pew, Pulpit and Pew, and those involving Pew and Pew, are waged against "the spiritual forces of evil" *(Eph. 6:12)*. What happens in many instances is someone or several fail to, "Take care," and in doing so, if for only a season, "have an evil, unbelieving heart that turns away from the living God" *(Heb. 3:12)*. Tragically, destructive conflict strikes at the finished work of Christ. Of Christ's finished work on the cross, Paul told the Church at Colossae, "There Christ defeated all powers and forces. He let the whole world see them being led away as prisoners when he celebrated his victory" *(Col. 2:15 CEV)*. It grieves God when those who are His in Christ behave in ways that name a lie Christ's victory on the cross. What the disruptive behavior of one of God's own children shows is this: "you are no longer walking in love" *(Rom. 14:15)*.

Again, Pulpit and Pew have a responsibility to be agents of correction in the household of God. That is part of what it means to be "instruments of grace." With corrective behavior such as speech goes a proper spirit. James wrote what seems to me to constitute such a spirit. He was advising against showing partiality. Which we know is a temptation and one we yield to when we enter a fray and take sides based on friendship, or do so to repay a debt of support for some past thing we wanted to get done. James said, "But if you show partiality, you commit sin and are convicted by the law as transgressors" *(Jas. 2:9)*. What are the saints to do? "So speak and so act as those who are to be judged by the law of liberty. For judgment will be without mercy to anyone who has shown no mercy; mercy triumphs over judgment" *(Jas. 2:12-13)*.

In dealing with people who have "a heavenly treasure in earthen vessels" we are called upon to give consideration to the nature of the vessel. For all of us, Pulpit and Pew, pastor and people are working on "sanctification." We have experienced the "instant aspect" of sanctification. We did so when we were "born again." But it is the "gradual aspect" that we are working on. The psalmist's words, "I have seen a limit to all perfection" *(Ps. 119:9b)*, apply to our sanctification in time. But that truth does not render invalid Jesus' mandate. "Be perfect, therefore, as your heavenly Father is perfect" *(Matt. 5:48)*. As all of God's children confess regarding perfection as they stand looking into the perfect face of Christ, "Not that I have already obtained this," and declaring, on the other hand, "but I press on to make it my own, because Christ Jesus has made me his own" *(Philp. 3:12)*. We make allowances for human weaknesses, and show mercy to those who do wrong. At the same time combatants in strife and perpetrators of disputes are to be held accountable for their conduct. Grace is present and available when we do wrong, but we are not to continue sinning because of grace's presence. "What then are we to say? Should we continue in sin in order that grace may abound? By no means! How can we who died to sin go on living in it?" *(Rom. 6:1-2)*

Christian Church members will not take delight and pleasure in the wrongs they do when their faith undergo momentary lapses. Instead they will grieve and repent *(cf. II Tim. 2:25-26)*.

Third, the members of the body of Christ who belong to one another are duty bound to affirm another reality. It is the reality of our common ownership by Christ that influences how we relate, treat and deal with one another. It is encumbent upon members of a family that they look out for one another. Whether the love shown is tough or tender, it will always be in the best interest of the other. For, Christ demands nothing less.

> *We do not live to ourselves, and we do not die to ourselves. If we live, we live to the Lord, and if we die, we die to the Lord; so then, whether we live or whether we die, we are the Lord's. For to this end, Christ died and lived again, so that he might be Lord of both the dead and the living.*

Rom. 14:7-9

Paul's assessment of relationships between those for whom Christ died and lives suggests the need for a mutual and common awareness that no one is alone in the Church. We belong to one another and we belong with one another. Superficial and artificial barriers to full enjoyment of what is ours in Christ have no right to survive and stand. Conflict in congregations is sometime the result of long standing differences and disputes between individual members and between families in the churches. After the reasons for the divisions have been forgotten, younger generations of persons sometimes continue the strife.

A pastor's past behavior related to a family in a congregation carried over into a later appointment to pastor another church. He was no longer a part of the offended family but his past actions were clung to by some members of his new church who were aware of what had taken place. The congregation's resistance to him was so great until his appointment was changed.

The above incident provides me an opportunity to establish that Pew must not deny Pulpit the benefit of grace. People who say of a pastor, "She can't tell me nothing, for I know what she has done," fail to allow that grace is sufficient for us all. A pastor whose faith lapsed should be permitted to preach faith until his faith is restored. Just as faith for Pew comes from hearing the word of God, the same holds for Pulpit. The Word of God proclaimed convicts all who have ears to hear. Whenever Christians refuse to hear, having ears to hear, divisions among Pew and Pew, or between families, as well as between Pulpit and Pew continue. Where believers understand that they are what they are by God's grace and His grace can change repentant Christians, there is no problem with turning loose the past. What may not be forgotten must of a certainty be forgiven. Where that is not done, we will be condemned before "the judgment bar of God." For by our refusal to forgive we make certain that we are not forgiven by our Father in heaven *(Matt. 6:14-15)*. How can we refuse to forgive when those who need it is a brother or a sister? In other words, all belong to Christ.

Some members excuse their refusal to let go of old grievances by claiming to know the persons they judge will not change. They may attempt to bolster their position by asking, "Can Ethiopians change their skin or leopards their spots?" *(Jer. 13:23)*. Even though the answer is "No", the question proves nothing in this regard. When the disciples asked Jesus, "Then who can be saved?" in response to his words regarding the difficulty for a rich man to be saved, he said, "For mortals it is impossible, but for God all things are possible" *(Matt. 19:23-26)*. A denial of the possibility for change in a human being is at the same time a denial of the efficacy of the power of God. Ultimately, God's interest is in changed hearts more than it is in changed behavior. Changed behavior may, indeed, and more likely than not, will revert to old behavior. It is the work of human efforts. But change of heart that results in new and different behavior is of God. It is not purely outward but is from the inside and is manifested outwardly. Peter must have had such in mind when he wrote, thus, "let your adornment be the inner self with the lasting beauty and quiet spirit, which is very precious in God's sight" *(I Pet. 3:4)*.

Pulpit and Pew may become over-zealous in directed teaching and in its follow through. They may become over-zealous out of self-righteousness. Rather than being merciful agents of corrective grace, they go for the spiritual jugular. They go for the kill. They become Creator and stop thinking of themselves as creature. Paul's words to the Romans as recorded in Romans 14:10-12 are sobering for those who hear.

> *"Why do you pass judgment on your brother or sister? Or you, why do you despise your brother or sister? For we will all stand before the judgement seat of God. For it is written,*
>
> > *'As I live, says the Lord, every knee shall bow to me, and every tongue shall give praise to God.'*
>
> *So then, each of us will be accountable to God."*

Four, purposeful prayer will work to prevent conflict and will resolve it should it occur. What is prayer? "Prayer is an invitation to God to intervene in our lives, to let His will prevail in our affairs; it is the opening of a window to Him in our will, an effort to make Him the

Lord of our soul."[12] What is prayer? "Prayer is the central avenue God uses to transform us."[13]

What is prayer? "Christian prayer ... is man's response to God's revelation."[14] What is prayer? "Prayer is a grace, an offer of God."[15] What is prayer? "Prayer is need finding a voice, embarrassment seeking relief, a friend in search of a Friend, knocking on a barred door, reaching out through the darkness."[16] St. Teresa of Avila answered the question with: "Prayer is the mortar that

---

[12]Abraham Joshua Heschel. *I Asked for Wonder* (N.Y. Crossroad Publishing Co., 1988), p. 28.

[13]Richard J. Foster. *Celebration of Discipline* (San Francisco: Harper and Row, 1988), p. 33.

[14]Olive Wyon. *Prayer* (Muhlenberg, Philadelphia, 1960), p. 16.

[15]Karl Barth. *Prayer* (Westminster, Philadelphia, 1952), p. 20.

[16]Charles L. Allen. *Prayer Changes Things* (Westwood, N.J., Fleming H. Revell, 1969), p. 10.

holds our house together."[17] And, finally, Fred C. Lofton answered, saying, "Prayer is the key to the Kingdom; ..."[18]

What is purposeful prayer? It is a believer taking God up on His offer of grace, showing trust in Him by asking Him to do a specific something. James the apostle touched on the negative of not being able to be specific. He wrote about doubting, and said, "the doubter, being double-minded and unstable in every way, must not expect to receive anything from the Lord" *(Jas. 1:8)*. A double-minded person lacks the focus that is necessary for effective praying. It telegraphs that the one who prays is not in sync with God's will. God's revelation in Jesus the Christ was focused in His redemptive purpose. Believers' response to His revelation means being as certain as Jesus was of his mission. Consequently, prayer for believers is asking God. "You do not have, because you do not ask" *(Jas. 4:2b)*. But it is not just asking. It is asking aright. "You ask and you do not receive, because you ask

---

[17]Quoted by Douglas V. Steere, *Dimensions of Prayer* (N.Y.: Harper and Row, 1963), p. 3.

[18]Fred C. Lofton. *When We Pray* (Elgin, Il: Progressive Baptist Publishing House, 1978), Preface.

wrongly, in order to spend what you get on your pleasures" *(Jas. 4:3)*. Purposeful praying is like a rifle shot, that is singular, instead of a shotgun blast that spreads and scatters.

Purposeful praying takes place where the praying person is being transformed. Where that is in process, prayer is not used in order to get so that what is received is used for purposes out of the realm of the Kingdom. Instead, what is received is to the glory of God.

Following the Transfiguration of Jesus, he came down from the mountain accompanied by Peter, James and John, the three disciples he took with him "up on the mountain to pray" *(Lk. 9:28)*. Once back on the plain, a man approached Jesus and told him that he brought his boy who "has a spirit" to his "disciples to cast it out." His pathetic words of accusation which were made to Jesus must have caused him grief. The boy's father said, "but they could not do so" *(Mk. 9:18)*. After Jesus cast out the spirit, his disciples asked him, "Why could we not cast it out? He said to them, "This kind can come out only through prayer" *(9:28-29)*.

Jesus identified the spirit as "This kind." The thing that is relevant to this discussion is that prayer is the only weapon that can cast out "This kind" of spirit. "This kind" caused considerable confusion in the boy and chaos around him. With the boy convulsing, being cast into fire and water, the spirit trying to destroy him, tranquility and peace were replaced with anxiety, confusion and fright. Bringing control to such a chaotic situation required going to the source with the one weapon capable of restoring calm. Prayer alone can cast out "This kind" of demon.

A congregation in conflict is experiencing the power of the demonic, which is the presence of a spirit alien to the Spirit of God. Why not engage prayer in the struggle to resolve it? Rather than be reactive, since we know that conflict is an enviable consequence of freedom of the will, why not use prayer proactively? Use prayer to create the type community where conflict is not comfortable. In as much as prayer is to bring transformation, strive for a praying Church in order that Pulpit and Pew may be transformed. "However, prayer is not panacea, no substitute for action. It is, rather, like a beam thrown from a flashlight before us into the darkness. It is in this light that we who grope, stumble, and climb, discover where we stand, what surrounds us, and the course which we should choose."[19]

A positive approach to purposeful prayer pro-actively employed is Paul's exhortation to the Church at Thessalonica. He told the Church, "pray without ceasing" *(I Thess. 5:17)*. Paul does not mean by "without ceasing" constant verbalizing prayers to God. It is not non-stop utterances of praise, adoration, confession, petition, intercession, supplication. What will make "prayer without ceasing" effective is two-fold. They are prayers for the community by the spiritual minded and prayer by the entire community for itself. In this regard, "pray without ceasing" ... implies constantly recurring prayer, growing out of a settled attitude for dependence on God. Whether words are uttered or not, lifting the heart to God while one is occupied with miscellaneous duties is the vital thing."[20]

Paul wrote in his Letter to the Romans, "For God, whom I serve with my spirit announcing the gospel of his

---

[19]Heschel, op. cit., p. 25f.

[20]*The Expository Bible Commentary*, Vol. 11 (Grand Rapids, MI: Zondervan, 1978), p. 291.

Son, is my witness that without ceasing I remember you always in my prayers" *(Rom. 1:9)*. This verse of scripture alludes to what immediately follows it, which is a specific purpose for which Paul prays "without ceasing." The relevance of this section to this discussion is to show that it is not foreign to Christian prayer for prayers to be focused. Focus in this discussion is on conflict within a community of faith. For Paul his focus was, "asking that by God's will I may somehow at last succeed in coming to you" *(10)*. Paul constantly prayed for that one thing. Yet, he left the outcome within "God's will."

It is safe to say that praying for peace in the Church, the local congregation and among the churches, is within the will of the God of peace *(Rom. 15:33)*. The things that make for dissension and disorder in the Church are of the devil, not of God. It is His plan to bring Satan down. As Paul said to the Romans, "The God of peace will shortly crush Satan under your feet" *(Rom. 16:20)*. While Christians, Pulpit and Pew, pastor and people, are called to war against the imps and instrument of Satan, Paul indicates that "God ... will shortly crush Satan." He is not just any God, but "the God of peace." Who is not the source of confusion and conflict, discord and division *(cf. II Cor. 11:12-15)*. He will "shortly crush Satan." Yet, the saints of God in Christ share with Him in the crushing. "For we are labourers together with God" *(I Cor. 3:9a)*. Moreover, "The God of peace will shortly crush Satan *under your feet.*" Though God will do the crushing, Paul instructed the Romans on their parts. He said to them, "I urge you, brothers and sisters, to keep an eye on those who cause dissensions and offenses, in opposition to the teaching that you have learned; avoid them. For such people do not serve our Lord Christ, but their own appetites, and by smooth talk and flattery they deceive the hearts of the simple minded" *(Rom. 16:17-18)*.

Too often conflict in congregations are not over matters of substance. Doctrinal and issues of faith are infrequently debated and rarely discussed. Of prominence as divisive issues are who will sign checks; who will run the revival; who will be paid what; who will have keys to the church; who authorized payment of that bill; who told you to buy the bulletins in the first place; whose job is it to count the collections; who picked out the caps for the Stewardesses; who told you to get that fixed; we don't pay the preacher on the Fifth Sunday; who is supposed to pay the guest preacher that the pastor had to preach in his place last Sunday. Trivial? It depends on who you ask. Divisive? Potentially, yes. How can prayer help? Remember, I am advocating a Church climate or an atmosphere in which discussion is allowed and expected. It is not a climate in which disagreement does not exist. It is one in which agreement to disagree exists. It is one where mutual respect for each other's person and position on issues exist. Such mutual respect is based on the truth that all are sisters and brothers in Christ. That all of us are His. He bought us with his blood and none of us have the right nor the freedom in Christ to treat any of us as though we are masters and others as slaves.

In congregations when the people of God meet for worship and for temporal matters the presence of the Spirit ought be acknowledged and recognized. Pulpit should by directed teaching instruct Pew in the sacred nature of assembling. This is not to be done in order to stifle debate but to let it be known that debate of issues and ideas, program concepts and plan suggestions must never degenerate to a level where proponents come under personal attack by opponents. Paul's mention of Alexandria to Timothy as a man who "did me great harm" *(II Tim. 4:14)*, is suggestive of a personal attack on Paul. "One good guess is that he had been responsible for the apostle's arrest and imprisonment."[21] Even so, Paul was confident that Alexander would be dealt with for his deeds. He would be dealt with in a way that is instructive for us who may be tempted to take matters in our own hands after a public confrontation with a member of Pulpit or Pew. In the time when for a moment we would forget, "Beloved, never avenge yourselves, but leave room for the wrath of God; for it is written, "Vengeance is mine, I will repay," says the Lord" *(Rom. 12:19)*. Remember Paul's commentary on Alexander's final outcome, "the Lord will pay him back for his deeds" *(II Tim. 4:14b)*.

Consistent with the nature of the body of Christ must be any discipline that is administered. "Do not be overcome by evil, but overcome evil with good" *(Rom. 12:21)*. That will be possible in a faith community where prayer is as natural as breathing.

---

[21]*The Expository Bible Commentary*, Vol. 11, op. cit., p. 415.

This approach puts love in practice. "Love does no wrong to a neighbor" *(Rom. 13:10)*. To paraphrase Paul, "If your brother is being injured by what you (do) eat, you are no longer walking in Love" *(Rom. 14:15)*. Love does not "rejoice in wrongdoing, but rejoices in the right" *(I Cor. 13:6)*. Possibly, the crowning advice on love in action is this: "Let all that you do be done in love" *(I Cor. 16:14)*. Love ought to be the way Christians live together in community *(Eph. 5:2)*. In that way the faith we claim to have is fulfilled. For as Paul said, "the only thing that counts is faith working through love" *(Gal. 5:6b)*. It is to this end that the Church where you meet must strive by praying for it. This display of love reveals trust in God. Praying transforms the one who prays, therefore, it fulfills Paul's desire to the "saints in Christ Jesus who are in Philippi" *(Philp. 1:1)*. His desire was for them to "be of the same mind, having the same love, being in full accord and of one mind" *(Philp. 2:2)*. Where such things are they will prove, "Who is wise and understanding" in that place.

Who is wise and understanding among you?
Show by your good life that your works are
done with gentleness born of wisdom. But if
you have bitter envy and selfish ambition in

*your hearts, do not be boastful and false to
the truth.*

*Such wisdom does not come down from
above, but is earthly, unspiritual, devilish.
For where there is envy and selfish
ambition, there will also be disorder and
wickedness of every kind. But the wisdom
from above is first pure, then peaceable,
gentle, willing to yield, full of mercy and
good fruits, without a trace of partiality or
hypocrisy. And a harvest of righteousness is
sown in peace for those who make peace.*
Jas. 3:13-18

Purposeful prayer is made by Christians who know
the differences between right behavior and wrong behavior.
Their prayers direct God to move the congregation as
Christ body to be like Christ, the head of the Church.
Only "holy behavior" is compatible with Christ's Church,
which is behavior out of the spirit of love. What makes
holy behavior love in action? Simply, God is love.
Behavior emanating from love is holy. After all, God is
holy. Our holiness is derived from God. In this way all
that is done is done in love *(Rom. 16:14)*. In no way is this
to be a one way love affair. Each and every member is to

"love one another with mutual affection" *(Rom. 12:10)*. Prayers by those who are of that awareness will be fruitful.

Five, involvement in service may be a deterrent or a corrective to congregational conflict. The New Testament is clear on ministry as the purpose for the Church. It begins with Jesus' own avowed purpose for being in the world. He said as much while in the synagogue in Nazareth.

> *The Spirit of the Lord is upon me, because*
> *he has anointed me to bring good news to*
> *the poor.*
>
> *He has sent me to proclaim release to the*
> *captives and recovery of sight to the blind,*
> *to let the oppressed go free, to proclaim the*
> *year of the Lord's favor.*
>   Lk. 4:18-19

When John the Baptist's disciples asked Jesus the question John sent them to ask, "Are you the one who is to come or are we to wait for another?," Jesus answered in terms of service to humankind.

> *Jesus had just then cured many people of*
> *diseases, plagues, and evil spirit, and had*
> *given sight to many who were blind. And he*
> *answered them, "Go and tell John what you*
> *have seen and heard: the blind receive their*

> *sight, the lame walk, the lepers are
> cleansed, the deaf hear, the dead are raised,
> the poor have good news brought to them.
> And blessed is anyone who takes no offense
> at me. "*
>
> Lk. 7:21-23

Jesus' commitment to ministry was so strong until he let nothing deter him nor detour him from reaching his goal. His goal was to finish the work God gave him to do. It was his passion, his food. An illustration of his commitment was what Jesus told his disciples when they returned with food to Jacob's well at Sychar. He said after declining their offer of food, "My food is to do the will of him who sent me and to complete his work" *(John 4:34)*.

The threat of Herod upon Jesus' life delivered by some Pharisees was insufficient to throw Jesus off schedule. He was a man with a definite sense of time. John's Gospel presents Jesus as one who was aware of his hour. At a wedding feast in Cana of Galilee, he told his mother, "My hour has not yet come" *(John 2:4)*. Later, in Jerusalem, Jesus announced, "The hour has come for the Son of Man to be glorified ..." *(John 12:23)*. His sense of destiny kept him on course. So, he gave a bone to be delivered to Herod by the same Pharisees who brought him a bone from Herod. He said, "Go and tell that fox for me, Listen, I am casting out demons and performing cures today and tomorrow, and on the third day I finish my work" *(Lk. 13:32)*.

From the Gospel of John we learn that Jesus sent his disciples into the world, just as God, the Father, had sent him into the world *(John 17:18)*. He sent them to do the works that he was doing. But he said, "the one who believes in me will also do the works that I do, and, in fact, will do greater works than these, because I am going to the Father" *(John 14:12)*. Doing of the "greater works" will not be done on human ingenuity and strength alone. They will be done through Jesus by the power of the Holy Spirit, whom Jesus promised *(cf. John 14:16, 26)*. The "greater works" are the fruits of the grace of God. His grace, being amazing in mercy and boundless in love, is able to effect great and marvelous things. As the branches are dependent upon the vine for sustenance and strength, the Church is dependent upon Christ. "Apart from me," said Jesus, "you can do nothing" *(John 15:5b)*. Jesus made the positive point, though conditional, "If you abide in me, and my words abide in you, ask for whatever you wish, and it will be done for you" *(John 15:7)*. So the works done by the Church, Pulpit and Pew, are done cooperatively with God.

I want to approach service or ministry from two related sides. It is a thesis of this sub-section that doing ministry will occupy Pulpit and Pew so completely that conflict will be prevented or dissolved if it exists. The first side that I will discuss is service from the institutional side of the Church. I do not mean that there are two churches, one invisible and spiritual and one visible and material. I understand the Church I see to be both. Yet, there are things that must be done to build up and maintain the institution. While these things may not be necessary to the being of the Church they are necessary for its well being.

As a young pastor, I drove some veteran pastors by automobile on several extended road trips. For me these trips were learning experiences. One thing that I learned was common or general in nature. What I learned was the kindred nature of the problems in churches without regard for their sizes. My small congregation was undergoing some of the same struggles and conflicts as were the larger congregations pastored by my mentoring colleagues.

I recall a bit of wisdom that came out as the two pastors were engaged in a verbal exchange. The two of them kind of celebrated their commonality on their position that a busy church is a peaceful church. As they said, "If you want to keep down trouble in the Church keep them working." I concluded from what they said that members who are kept busy are too busy to fight.

The busyness which they alluded to were things done to maintain the institution. By and large their references were to "money raising." Anyone familiar with African American churches knows about, "Rallies," "Big Days," "putting on a Program," "Drives." My two veteran colleagues believed that by keeping members immersed in the process associated with raising money kept them from fussing and fighting among themselves. Having been involved in money raising, I am familiar with the process. It involves initial planning, inclusive of an organization, the setting of a date, a financial goal and a theme. Once the Pulpit announces the drive, a frenzy develops, especially when the effort is competitive. Members often become totally wrapped up in the fund raising.

I believe that Jesus was on the side of busyness. His parable of the laborers in the vineyard may be applied to support his dislike for idleness. The laborers who were hired at different times of the day, early in the morning, at nine o'clock, noon, three and five o'clock, were all paid the same wage at day's end. Now, what could be more noble than the landowner's disdain for idleness which caused him to risk criticism by treating all the workers equal? As long as the workers were busy, they did not fuss. It was only after work that they criticized the landowner. While they worked, their busyness occupied their minds and their mouths *(cf. Matt. 20:1-16)*.

A challenge to the practicality of the "keep them busy" philosophy is whether it can be done continually. The success of a financial drive opens a congregation to the possibility of either excessive pride or depressive gloom. Jesus' own disciples manifested pride to an apparently excessive level upon returning from a successful mission. Luke reports that they returned with joy, saying to Jesus, "Lord, in your name even the demons submit to us." Jesus sought to get them to understand that there was something more important than success. He said, "do not rejoice at this, that the spirits submit to you, but rejoice that your names are written in heaven" *(Lk 10:17-20)*. Jesus' words, "the spirits submit to you," reveal that their successful mission could make them think that the power belonged to them. What was of first importance was their own salvation, "your names are written in heaven."

On the other hand, depressive gloom is what came over Elijah after his successful triumph on Mount Carmel over the prophets of Baal. After Elijah's spectacular victory, he became like Dietrick Bonhoeffer's "beaten army coming back from victory already achieved." Elijah's depression turned him in to himself, to the point that he thought that the Israelites "are seeking my life, to take it away" *(I Kings 19:10)*. After his great victory, which the Lord won for him, Elijah became self-absorbed. It was the Lord and not Elijah who rained fire down from heaven which consumed the altar and the sacrifice *(I Kings 18:38)*.

From both examples, the disciples and the prophet Elijah, the danger of success is the possibility of the self moving into the center as God's replacement. With the self in the center, the scene is set again for conflict, which is a replay, or a re-turn of the Adam and Eve syndrome. After they took center stage where they upstaged God with the exercise of free will, they defied God and ate of the tree of knowledge of good and evil. When accosted by God, they broke the harmony that prevailed in the Garden of Eden by accusing another, Eve, or the serpent, for their behavior *(Gen. 3:8-13)*.

If success has its downside, would the failure of a "Rally" or a "Drive" mean there is no danger of resulting conflict? I think not. A case in point are Jesus' disciples who failed in their efforts to cast a spirit out of a boy. When Jesus came down from the Mount of Transfiguration with Peter, James, and John, they found the other nine disciples with a great crowd around them, as they argued with some scribes. Jesus asked the nine disciples, "What are you arguing about with them?" They did not answer quickly. So a man from the crowd answered, fingering their failure to cast the demon out of his son *(Mk. 9:14-29)*. Once the disciples failed in their attempt to do something, they should have been equipped to do, they resorted to subterverge, they argued.

I do not deny that busyness may serve as a temporary panacea for conflict. But I do deny its power to permanently keep conflict down.

A second level of service is the use of the gifts of the Spirit. I do not want to convey the idea that the first level of busyness just discussed is in no way related to the second level. Money is necessary to the well being of the institutional church. Engagement in mission and in ministries takes money. I am acutely aware that there are members, Pulpit and Pew, who regard "raising money" as nothing more than making the Lord's house of prayer a den of thieves *(cf. Lk. 19:46)*. Nonetheless, not every congregation is committed to tithing, nor to systematic giving. I know of congregations with membership so small until with all members tithing the proceeds would be insufficient to fund the church's budget. Also, money-raising abilities may indicate gifts of the Spirit. I am not one to limit gifts of the Spirit to those listed in the Pauline epistles *(cf. Rom. 12:6-8; I Cor. 12:4-11; Eph. 4:11)*. I believe the same Spirit who gave gifts as they were necessary for the apostolic community gives to His Church in the 20th Century according to His will and purpose. Some if not all churches in the 20th Century may have budgetary requirements that churches in the 1st Century did not have. As the Church of God in Christ, why would God leave them without the endowment of gifts that equip them for community and for service? I do not accept the idea that God's Spirit has ceased equipping the saints for relevant ministries.

My approach to the second level will avoid discussing the specifics related to gifts of the Spirit. I am committed to the belief that if Christians are brought to a higher understanding of their calling, one that includes yet transcends the Church as institution, their busyness in ministry takes precedence over quarrels and disputes associated with "keeping and running the store." What errands are important and who runs them are, then, more significant than who keeps or who runs the store. The former are ministries and the latter are purely maintenance kinds of things by church members.

The Christian life is a life of spirituality. And, "Spirituality, reveals Paul, is a life guided and directed by the Holy Spirit. Concretely, it is life in and from

community, conformity to Christ for the sake of others."[22]
For busyness to be spiritually satisfying, what is done must
be "life in and for community." Life in community is life
in and of the spirit. The entire and complete existence of
all who are in Christ is new *(II Cor. 5:17)*. It is human
beings in "conformity to Christ." When Paul said, "I have
been crucified with Christ; and it is no longer I who live,
but it is Christ who lives in me. And the life I now live in
the flesh I live by faith in the Son of God, who loved me
and gave himself for me" *(Gal. 2:19b-20)*, he was not saying
the Spirit had no part. For Paul said, "Now the Lord is
the Spirit" *(II Cor. 3:17)*. While Paul had died with Christ on
the cross, he had been made alive by the Spirit *(cf. Rom.
8:10)*. At the center of Paul's life in the body was Christ.
With Christ at the center, Paul was no longer dependent
upon anything else, nor anyone else. He had prayed for
the thorn in his flesh to be removed and God refused, with
God saying, "My grace is sufficient for you, for power is
made perfect in weakness," and Paul responding, "So, I

---

[22]Winter, Gibson. "America In Search Of Its Soul,"
Theology Today (Princeton, N.J., Jan. 1996, Vol. 4), p. 472.

will boast all the more gladly of my weaknesses, so that the power of Christ may dwell in me" *(II Cor. 12:8-9)*.

So, when Paul said, "it is Christ who lives in me," he acknowledged total dependency upon the Spirit. By virtue of being under the Spirit's power, Paul lived and so do we, Pulpit and Pew, in conformity to Christ. For the Spirit is in sync with God's will *(cf. Rom. 8:26-27)*. God's will is community. From the outset of creation God intended community. The orderliness of His creation is legend. He looked at "everything that he had made and it was very good" *(Gen. 1:31)*. In the thought of Aristotle, "good" means that everything served the purpose for which God made it. The proper working of all things meant harmony and peace prevailed. So it is with the church, God's faith community. When each part of the church "is working properly, promotes the body's growth in building itself up in love" *(Eph. 4:16b)*.

Pulpit and Pew called into community are gifted for community. It is to that end that gifts are given by the Spirit. Life in community decreases the stress factor which contributes to deterioration of spiritual health. God's will for His creation is health and wholeness of being. We can verify that by the ways Jesus lived his life on earth. He ministered to people by making life more bearable. He relieved them from their pain, suffering, and disabilities. Jesus' ministry began focused in community. "Now after John was arrested, Jesus came to Galilee, proclaiming the good news of God, and saying, "The time is fulfilled, and the kingdom of God has come near; repent, and believe in the good news" *(Mk. 1:14-15)*. The kingdom of God is the ultimate community. In it God reigns. Its existence is proximate in history and time. But there will come endtime when there will be "a new heaven and a new earth" where the "home of God is among mortals. He will dwell among them as their God; they will be his peoples, and God himself will be with them, he will wipe every tear from their eyes. Death will be no more; mourning and crying and pain will be no more, for the first things have passed away" *(Rev. 21:1-4)*.

Second, for service to be meaningful it must have measurable goals. It has been said that a road that leads nowhere is difficult to build. Human beings want to feel that what they do in life counts, that it has meaning. In matters spiritual, measurements are hard to come by. As a young pastor, I was disturbed because I seemed to be making little if any progress in the ways my congregation behaved in business meetings, participated in outreach ministries and in teaching-learning sessions. When I shared my frustration with a more experienced pastor, he said to me, "Remember what Jesus said happens in heaven when one soul is saved? Well, consider your work a blessing if you make a positive difference in one person's life."

Making a positive difference in another's life makes ministry meaningful. Paul staked the authenticity of his apostleship on his impact on the lives of believers in Christ. He told the saints at Corinth, "you are the seal of my apostleship in the Lord" *(I Cor. 9:2)*. Apparently, some questioned Paul's apostleship. He told the Corinthians that he did not need letters of commendation to them or from them. Such letters were customary for emissaries traveling into areas where they were not known. Paul's reason for not needing such letters, he explained thus to the Corinthians, "You yourselves are our letter, written on our hearts, to be known and read by all; and you show that you are a letter of Christ, prepared by us, written not with ink but with the Spirit of the living God, not on tablets of stone but on tablets of human hearts" *(II Cor. 3:2-3)*.

When Paul wrote to Timothy and said, "I have fought the good fight, I have finished the race, I have kept the faith" *(II Tim. 4:7)*, the "good fight" that Paul had fought included his ministry to the Gentiles. His fight was good because of "letters" such as the Corinthians. He had down times such as he wrote of to the Galatians. He said, "My little children, for whom I am again in the pain of childbirth until Christ is formed in you. I wish I were present with you now and could change my tone, for I am perplexed about you" *(Gal. 4:19-20)*.

The down times Paul had in ministry were counter-balanced by up times. In contrast to the Churches of Galatia, he wrote "To all the saints in Christ Jesus who are in Philippi" and said, "I thank my God every time I remember you, constantly praying with joy in every one of my prayers for all of you, because of your sharing in the gospel from the first day until now" *(Philp. 1:1, 3-5)*.

Paul was convinced that he was in Christ. He knew when it happened, where it happened, and how it happened *(Acts 22:-16)*. Beyond that, Paul was equally certain of his calling to be apostle to the Gentiles *(Gal. 1:11-17)*. Paul measured his successes by those who accepted Christ Jesus as Lord. He did not count numbers, he remembered persons. Their growth and the ways they expressed their faith in keeping and maintaining community which are marks of growth. There is contagion in Paul's listing of the names, in his epistles, of persons who had come into the faith and who had grown in it *(cf. Rom. 16:1-16)*.

Gifts come from the Spirit to be used to the glory of Christ through the benefit of others. The gifts may be cooking, cleaning, driving a bus, serving as a captain for a Rally, for leading, singing, playing a musical instrument, counseling, encouraging, lecturing, teaching, preaching, making peace, lifting up others.

Chapter IV
ATTITUDES AND APPROACHES FOR DEALING WITH CONFLICT, REVISITED

First, for ministry to serve as a preventive or corrective for conflict, Pulpit and Pew must intentionally address the issue. In other words, Pulpit and Pew, must name what they are going against. Conflict has been identified, but its shape or form takes on specificity according to the particular context. While general counsel on dealing with conflict has been discussed, dealing with specific instances will be discussed now. By general counsel, I mean the discussion of the meaning of the church. To call attention to the God who purchased the church with the blood of His Son, Jesus the Christ, and to discuss the Church as the body of Christ were intentionally done as deterrents and correctives. I am of the opinion that knowledge and understanding of the nature of God, Christ, and the Church, and of proper behavior expected of the saved will result in people doing what they ought to do.

Pew and Pulpit must not be naive about the people who populate the Church. It is fair to say that not only are there good and bad persons in the Church, but there are persons in the Church who themselves are both good and bad. Goethe wrote in the first part of *Faust*:

> *"Two souls, alas, are housed within my breast,*
>
> *And each will wrestle for the mastery there.* "[23]

By good and bad I mean there are Christians who live and act or behave properly as a Christian ought, and there are Christians who do not live, act, behave, properly as a Christian ought. Then, there are Christians who live, act and behave both as they ought and ought not. They go from the one to the other. The latter fall into Goethe's apt description of human beings.

If Christians waver and go this way and then the other, who among them are in position to serve the preventive and corrective roles? Except for habitual trouble makers and hell raisers the roles may change from one Christian to another. Let me see if in considering something Paul wrote, a principle of interpretation may be

---

[23]Quoted by E. H. Robertson. *Man's Estimate of Man* (Richmond, VA: Muhlenberg, 1958), p. 11.

found. Paul said, "Indeed, there have to be factions among you, for only so will it become clear who among you is genuine" *(I Cor. 11:19)*.

"There is no doubt that the *genuine* are those who hold to the meaning of the Supper within a sense of *community*, demonstrated in sensitivity to one another."[24] The genuine faction in every case is the one that is on the side of unity as expressed in community, and show what side they are on by their sensitivity to others and their commitment to the common good.

It is an easy matter to label others hypocrites when they seem at one moment to be bent on destroying community and the next moment preserving it. But the issue is not the specific issue, rather, it is what at the time best serves community.

Second, Pulpit and Pew must be clear about their stance on compromise. Allow me to introduce what seems like contradictory behavior carried out by the apostle Paul. His behavior revolved around circumcision which, as anyone knows who reads his epistles, he believed it to be

---

[24]*The Broadman Bible Commentary*, Vol. 10 (Nashville: Broadman Press, 1970), p. 356.

a *no-thing*. He wrote, "if you let yourselves be circumcised, Christ will be of no benefit to you" *(Gal. 5:2)*. Christ for Paul was of more value than any gain he had made in life *(Philp. 3:7-11)*. Yet, in spite of Paul's feeling about circumcision, according to Luke, "Paul wanted Timothy to accompany him; and he took him and had him circumcised ..." *(Acts 16:3)*. Why did Paul do it? Luke said, "because of the Jews who were in those places *(Lystra and Iconium)*, for they all knew his father was a Greek" *(3b)*.

On the other hand, Paul resisted efforts in Jerusalem to circumcise Titus. He looked upon the efforts of "false believers" as attempts to "enslave us." For Christ had made them free *(Gal. 5:2-5)*.

Why did Paul take different positions in the two instances? It could be that he had Timothy circumcised because, "To circumcise him would greatly increase his usefulness to Paul, for it would disarm suspicion among the Jews in the new districts which he was planning to visit. Moreover, we have hints in his letters that Paul would not have considered such action culpably inconsistent if he felt that it would contribute to the success of his gospel."[25]

It might be argued that Paul had Timothy circumcised because Paul's purpose or mission as a minister of the gospel to Gentiles *(Gal. 2:1-17)*, took precedent over particular situations. Now, when Paul's behavior is placed within the context of his commitment to ministry, we come up with an explanation of his behavior relative to Timothy. Paul said, "For though I am free with respect to all, ... I have become all things to all people, that I might by all means save some" *(I Cor. 9:19, 22b)*.

The guiding principle for Paul's behavior was his ministry and the good of the gospel. In a sense community welfare and well being were paramount.

When Pulpit and Pew take their stances on issues in the congregation they are genuine to the extent they serve community, which means that almost no one serves community all of the time. Nonetheless, Paul called Alexander by name, thereby identifying him as the one

---

[25]*The Interpreter's Bible*, Vol. 9 (New York: Abingdon, 1954), p. 211.

who "did me great harm" *(II Tim. 4:14)*. Retaliation was not on Paul's agenda. He said, "The Lord will pay him back for his deeds" *(14b)*. The counsel Paul gave to Timothy in dealing with Alexander was, "You also must be aware of him" *(15)*.

Paul identified trouble makers in Philippi calling them "the dogs" ... "the evil workers." They caused trouble by practicing circumcision *(Philp. 3:2-4)*. Paul addressed the problem by referencing himself as one who was circumcised on the eighth day *(5)*. But the weight of his argument fell on what he gave up as a Jew "because of Christ" *(7)*. His appeal was to grace through faith rather than works. It was through reason that Paul presented his case.

Third, Pulpit and Pew must know the difference between an attack on them personally and the programs they espouse and support. Jesus was attacked on both, himself, personally, and the program he championed. From the outset of his ministry, on the very day that he announced the inauguration of his ministry came under attack. You will recall that the synagogue congregation in Nazareth was receptive to Jesus as long as he read from "the scroll of the prophet Isaiah" *(Lk. 4:17)*. Reading was a detached exercise. As long as he just read, or read, only, the congregation was alright, it was at ease. When he sat down, "the eyes of all in the synagogue were fixed on him" *(Lk. 4:20b)*. Then, after sitting, Jesus made a personal claim. He injected himself into what he had read. He said, "Today this scripture has been fulfilled in your hearing" *(Lk. 4:21)*. At first, the congregation responded in a way that Luke described in these words, "All spoke well of him and were amazed at the gracious words that came from his mouth" *(Lk. 4:22)*. In the almost same breath, they asked, "Is not this Joseph's son?" Their question evidenced a conclusion about Jesus that stopped far short of understanding him as God's Son. To them he was simply Joseph's son.

Jesus was attacked at home by the folks who knew his family. They attacked what he did and said because of who his family was. He could not possibly know what he talked about and what he did because they knew he was a nobody. They knew his father and his mother, his brothers and his sisters. They asked, "Where then did this man get all this?" *(Matt. 13:56)*.

On the other hand, Jesus was attacked at the heart of his ministry. In a sense, critics attacked his program. The heart of his ministry was the proclamation of the good news of the kingdom *(cf. Matt. 4:17)*. Jesus proclaimed the good news of the kingdom of God in words and in deeds. Relative to word proclamation Jesus said, "I must proclaim the good news of the kingdom of God to the other cities also; for I was sent for this purpose" *(Lk. 4:43)*.

Also, Jesus proclaimed the kingdom of God with deeds and miracles of healing. The scribes from Jerusalem who came to his home accused him of having Beelzebub and of casting out demons "by the ruler of demons" *(Mk. 3:22)*. Jesus responded to both groups with reasoned explanations.

With his hometown folks who questioned his identity to show them any signs, he cited two prophets of the Old Testament. Both refused to do signs for their own people; Elijah and Elisha both performed mighty works for outsiders *(Lk. 4:24-27)*. Jesus who had done mighty works in Capernaum did not accede to the requests from the people in Nazareth.

For the scribes who questioned the nature of his program by identifying Jesus with Beelzebub, he reasoned that, "if Satan has risen up against himself and is divided, he cannot stand, but his end has come. But no one can enter a strong man's house and plunder his property without first tying up the strong man; then indeed the house can be plundered" *(Mk. 3:26-27)*. Jesus had entered a strong man's house by the miracles and the mighty works He had done. He plundered Satan's house. For the evil spirits were Satan's house.

Reasoned explanations do not always succeed, particularly, when the attacks are emotional. While such responses to emotion-packed attacks are worth trying, it is difficult to reason with those who are biased and prejudiced. The people in Jesus' hometown were biased against him because they knew he could not possibly be anybody. He was a no-body in Nazareth.

Pulpit may know what it is like to be set upon from an emotional base. It happens. Attacks may be upon Pulpit's person, or Pulpit's program. Either or both have no basis in fact. But that does not matter. At the root of opposition lies non-acceptance of the person. Just as Jesus was never accepted in some instances, Pulpit will not be accepted. So, what do you do?

One, Jesus was convinced that his life and his work were set on a solid foundation. An illustration of foundations was given by Jesus. He told of wise and foolish builders who built their houses on a rock and on sand, respectively. The difference between the two was the wise man heard and acted on Jesus' words and the foolish man heard but did not act on Jesus' words. When the forces of opposition attacked in the forms of rain, floods, and wind, only the house built on rock stood *(Matt. 7:24-29)*. Which suggests that Jesus, too, stood on God's words and acted on them. In his confrontation with the devil in the wilderness, Jesus used the Holy Scriptures as his basis for resistance *(Matt. 4:1-11)*.

Pulpit and Pew ought to operate, if you will, from a solid foundation. I do not mean they ought to have a scripture for everything they do. I do mean that the spirit of God's Word should undergird their lives and their actions. I think Bible literalists would be hard pressed to show that Jesus lived and acted in accordance with the letter of the law. It is common fare to say that he fulfilled it, or, that he accomplished all of it *(cf. Matt. 5:17-20)*. Yet, it must be admitted that by Jesus quoting the law, thus, "it was said of those in ancient times, "You shall not murder;" and whoever murders shall be subject to judgment," and following with, "But I say to you that if you are angry with a brother or sister, you will be liable to judgment; ..." *(Matt. 5:21-22)*, Jesus put a human face on his interpretation of the law.

To establish our lives and our actions on the Word of God means to be and to do in the spirit of Jesus the Christ, who was the Word made flesh *(John 1:14)*. Jesus put human beings ahead of the requirements of the Law. The laws associated with the Sabbath were observed religiously. But Jesus said, "the Son of Man is lord of the Sabbath" *(Matt. 12:8)*. When that claim is combined with Jesus declaration, The Sabbath was made for humankind, and not humankind for the Sabbath" *(Mk. 2:27)*, it becomes clear why he risked inciting opposition to him doing good and helping individuals on the Sabbath *(cf. Mk. 3:1-6; Lk. 6:1-5; 13:10-17)*.

A principle that stands in all situations and under every circumstance is service of "the common good." I have already said that God's original design for creation was community. He sent forth Jesus into the world to restore what sin had torn down. Jesus' vision of community took the form of "the kingdom of God." I am not equipped to argue the relationship of "the body of Christ" to God's kingdom. But according to my understanding, "the body of Christ" is only a proximation of what the Kingdom of God will be. The Church as the body of Christ is populated with saints having clay feet. Yet, in spite of our imperfections we are the best God has in the world. Christ's body in the world is like concentric circles. It moves outward from the center which is Christ himself and with every convert the center expands outward into the world. God's will is that the good of everyone within the circle be served. It is, therefore, the responsibility of every member of the Church to serve the good of all of the members, together. From the apostolic church onward, an undergirding principle is this: "All who believed were together and had all things in common; ..." *(Acts 2:44).*

The question that is consistent with the word of God is: What action on my part serves love best in this instance? What serves love best serves the common good.

So if I am attacked as a person, I do not retaliate *(Matt. 5:39)*. Even I may be in the way of what is good for the whole.

Also, "my program" may be attacked. Why should it be exempt from scrutiny? If it is "my program," or Pulpit's program for Pew, why shouldn't Pew have the privilege of input? Should Pew be expected to support a program on which they had nothing to say? From the perspective of love, Pulpit must remember, love "does not insist on its own way" *(I Cor. 13:5)*. All who make up a congregation "are God's servants, working together" *(I Cor. 3:9)*. Also, Pew must be mindful in resisting Pulpit's program, "love is not envious or boastful or arrogant or rude, ... it does not rejoice in wrongdoing" *(I Cor. 13:4-6)*. Love "rejoices in the truth" *(I Cor. 13:6b)*. Truth is what is whole and complete. To do love is to do what serves the whole congregation.

Two, Jesus was focused. From the temptation in the wilderness onward, Jesus' life was focused in a mission that would lead to his death. I wrote earlier about his commitment to ministry. Now I emphasize his singular dedication to his Father's business *(Lk. 2:49 KJV)*. Paul referring to himself said, "this one thing I do" *(Philp. 3:13b)*, which, if we are honest, we will acknowledge that focusing on one thing is very difficult. Yet, Paul confessed that is what he did. And my position is that is what Jesus did. Luke's word describe what I mean when he wrote about Jesus' determination. "When the days drew near for him to be taken up, ..." *(Lk. 9:51)*. Then, he described Jesus' resolve thus, "he steadfastly set his face to go to Jerusalem" (51b). The late Bishop William Yancey Bell of the Christian Methodist Episcopal Church said the meaning is, "he set his face like a flint." His face was hardened with determination. Looking neither to the right nor to the left, he faced straight ahead to Jerusalem. What powerful symbolic meaning!

Pulpit and Pew that would deal with opposition and with conflict must be focused. Without focus, Pulpit cannot provide leadership and Pew cannot exemplify the nature and meaning of the body of Christ. Unfocused persons are like the "double minded" James the apostle referred to. Of whom he said, they "must not expect to receive anything from the Lord" *(Jas. 1:7)*. Of course double mindedness is not an incurable condition. By drawing near to God and by purifying "your hearts" *(Jas. 4:8)*, the condition is curable.

What does focus have to do with dealing with conflict? It occupies the mind, thereby, preventing Pulpit and Pew from becoming obsessed with it. Doesn't this imply a kind of head in the sand reaction? I think not. First, any pastor or church member who is distracted by every brush fire in a church will spend a lifetime putting out brush fires. Second, aren't there some fights that belong to God? When Paul told Timothy that at his first defense all of his human companions "deserted me," he said, also, "But the Lord stood by me." Not only that, Paul also said, "The Lord will rescue me from every evil attack and save me for his heavenly kingdom" *(II Tim. 4:16-18)*.

It is often concluded by believers in God in Christ that they "must do something" when facing adversarial circumstances. But it is still true that in seeming impossible situations the faithful can do no better than "stand still and see the salvation of the Lord" *(Exod. 14:13 KJV)*.

Three, Jesus was convicted in his belief that victory would come out of seeming defeat. Sometimes an inexperienced pastor can not tolerate the thought of losing a fight for something he or she thinks is best for a church. The ideas may not always be their's but sometimes, if approved, they negatively affect the common good. After Pulpit expresses opposition, the Pew may give its vote of approval. Admittedly, Pulpit may become more than disappointed. Even become angry. How should Pulpit handle it? Take it on the chin. After all, the Pew voted what was the will of the people. Later on, Pulpit may adopt as its response something that I heard from the late Presiding Elder W. C. Crenshaw. He said regarding his way of dealing with unwanted situations, "I've learned to hold my nose and keep on going."

What Jesus can teach us is that defeat in a battle does not mean the loss of the war. In his pre-Calvary life, Jesus tried to teach his disciples that the suffering he must undergo in Jerusalem, and not even the death he must die, meant his end. He always added, somewhat as an addendum, and one that seemed to get lost, "and on the third day be raised" *(Matt. 16:21)*. He said in a way the victory comes out of defeat. Hope would rise from the decay of death.

Pulpit and Pew can grasp the compelling quality in Jesus' willingness to suffer and die in order to reach a new and higher level of spirituality from the author of the Letter To The Hebrews. The author wrote, saying, "and let us run with perseverance the race that is set before us, looking to Jesus the pioneer and perfecter of our faith, who for the sake of the joy that was set before him endured the cross, disregarding its shame, and has taken his seat at the right hand of the throne of God" *(Heb. 12:1b-2)*.

Jesus endured the negative and the bad, the shame of dying on a cross *(cf. Deut. 21:22-23)*, by looking beyond it. He kept his eyes on "the joy that was set before him." What he went through he did so in order to reach a goal. By holding out and holding on Jesus reached his destination, "the right hand of the throne of God."

Joseph's words to his brothers provide a different insight for use in explaining why difficulties come into the way of Pulpit and Pew. After summoning his brothers back to Egypt, where this time he revealed himself to them and to his father, Joseph said, "And now do not be distressed, or angry with yourselves because you sold me here; for God sent me before you to preserve life" *(Gen. 45:5)*. Divine providence was at work in what was a dastardly deed. Behind human acts, good and bad, is a plan at work; God's plan. So, as Joseph said, "Even though you intended to do harm to me, God intended it for good, in order to preserve a numerous people, as he is doing today" *(Gen. 50:20)*. Out of what the King James Version calls "evil," God brings good.

From conflict in a congregation God can bring good, provided Pulpit and Pew open themselves to divine possibility. The biblical view of "various trials" is that with rejoicing, that is, by not allowing trials to turn us towards despair, they contribute to the genuine-ness of our faith *(cf. I Pet. 1:6-7)*. According to James, "the testing of your faith produces endurance; and let endurance have its full effect, so that you may be mature and complete, lacking in nothing" *(Jas. 1:3-4)*. Where conflict is regarded as testing for individuals, or for congregations, with the proper spirit it moves them toward maturity. Proper spirit involves accepting dissidents, antagonists and hell raisers with understanding, willing to discuss with them differences that exist and to forgive where wrong has been done.

Fourth, there are times when Pulpit and Pew should approach the issue head-on. Occasions present themselves when individuals in conflict must meet in a head-to-head, eyeball-to-eyeball confrontation. The object of the discussion is the accused individual but the subject is the issue in conflict. Take Paul and Cephas for example. Paul wrote, "But when Cephas came to Antioch, I opposed him to his face" *(Gal. 2:11)*.

The confrontation here was one on one. Paul took on Peter in a head-to-head, eyeball-to-eyeball encounter. There was a lot at stake. In a sense, Paul's ministry to the Gentiles was in the background. Personally, Cephas' integrity was in the balance. Would it be found wanting? Paul said without reservation that the reason he opposed Cephas was, "because he stood self-condemned." Cephas along with James and John affirmed Paul's ministry to the Gentiles. Cephas, according to Paul, "used to eat with the Gentiles." But after "certain people came from James ... he drew back and kept himself separate for fear of the circumcision faction" *(Gal. 2:11-12)*.

The Paul-Cephas encounter did not take place in a corner. It was personal but it was not private. Paul said what he had to say "before them all" *(14a)*. Thus, Cephas' behavior was made even more embarrassing. One of the "acknowledged pillars" *(Gal. 2:9)*, had behaved hypocritically. He showed little, if any, courage regarding the circumcision party. Which is somewhat reminiscent of his lack of courage in Pilate's courtyard when he denied Jesus after being confronted by a young woman *(Lk. 22:54-62)*.

The Paul-Cephas encounter did not take place over a trivial matter. For Paul, at issue was justification "through faith in Jesus Christ" *(Gal. 2:16)*. Salvation by grace through faith was the centerpiece of Paul's theology. Salvation, therefore, is a gift of God in Christ Jesus. Circumcision was a matter of keeping the law, and for Paul it was works righteousness.

Head-to-head, eyeball-to-eyeball confrontations which are always potentially, volatile, should be on clearly defined issues. They should be over matters and issues of substance, even issues that are larger than the question. As was noted relative to the Paul-Cephas confrontation, circumcision was the question, but salvation by grace through faith was the larger issue. Grace versus the law as the means of salvation was the ultimate issue. At another level, Paul had to get "this thing off his chest." So may we who are burdened by a wrong committed against the faith, or against us, personally. Our good health may depend on getting "this thing" over with.

Fifth, Pulpit must learn to be something of a chameleon in dealing with church members. I mean pretty much what Paul wrote, saying, "I have become all things to all people, that I might by all means save some" *(I Cor. 9:22b)*. Making the attitudinal adjustments necessary "to please everyone" *(cf. I Cor. 10:31-33)*, is not easy. When I served as a local church pastor, a member asked me how was it possible to visit twelve to fifteen patients in six different hospitals, many of whom, were very ill, and be prepared for what I encountered in each patient. I explained that it was not always easy to do. But over time and after visiting members confined as patients in hospitals, I had become sensitive about transporting the effect one patient had upon me to the patient I visited next. So I would make it my business to order my countenance before entering each room. What it amounted to was I entered each patient's room prepared to encounter that person as an individual. Conflict in a congregation is caused more often than not by an individual. Individuals, even groups of individuals, may be involved but it is normally fueled and led by an individual. Such individuals cause and continue conflict in pretty much the same fashion as was the behavior of "younger widows" which Paul described. He said, "they learn to be idle, but also gossips and busy bodies, saying what they should not say" *(I Tim. 5:13)*. Modern gossipers have telephones, faxes, and God forbid, e-mail. Let us look at some of the types of trouble makers with which Pulpit must deal and suggest some responses to each.

Why Pulpit? The pastor is the leader of the congregation. There are other leaders but there are none who are out front of Pulpit. Sometime an individual in the office of pastor may not have caught up with the role and responsibility, or the authority and power, or the expectations and demands of the office, but all of these are in the office of pastor or Pulpit. Sometime conflict ensues where Pew is out of touch with the role of Pulpit and attempts to take charge. Conflict ensues in many instances not because pastor rises up in resistance to those who would take charge, but because others of the Pew, on the one hand, recognize how wrong the efforts are, and, because on the other hand, there is confusion in the congregation due to a lack of clarity as to who is in charge.

There is an old saying which holds that when God got ready to deliver Israel from Egyptian bondage, he selected one person, Moses. Had he chosen a committee, the saying continues, the Israelites would still be in Egypt. As a follow up on this, I will mention something that happened when the people tried to supplant their leader. In this case, while Moses was on the mountain conferring with God, the people convinced Aaron to make them gods which would go before them. God was ready to destroy His own people until Moses convinced Him otherwise. God's interpretation of the meaning of "the molded calf" was that they had rejected His sovereign leadership, which was what the Israelites told Aaron. They said, "Come, make us gods that shall go before us; for as for this Moses, the man who brought us up out of the land of Egypt, we do not know what has become of him" *(Exod. 32:1b NIV)*.

Heretofore, "the Lord went before them by day in a pillar of cloud to lead the way, and by night in a pillar of fire to give them light, so as to go by day and night" *(Exod. 13:21)*.

Moses confronted Aaron and asked, "What did this people do to you that you have brought so great a sin upon them?" Aaron put it on the people, saying to Moses, "you know the people, that they are bent on evil." The pertinent fact may be the commentators insight. He wrote, thus, "When Moses saw that the people were running wild for Aaron had let them run wild, to the derision of their enemies" *(Exod. 32:21, 22b, 25)*. Discipline is part and parcel of what Pulpit is called to do. I know that in some Church circles it is not correct to set the Pulpit up as being in charge of the Pew. But as the one gifted by God to be Pastor, Pulpit has responsibility for the Pew and is held accountable for carrying out the responsibility *(cf. Ezek. 33:1-11; 34:7-10; Zech. 11:4-17; Eph. 4:11-16)*.

Chapter V
PULPIT UNDER ATTACK

Pulpit is often the object and subject of attacks by Pew. I suggest that the office of Pastor makes it a lightning rod for the Pew to set upon. At this time, I will point out some types of those in the Pew who attack the Pulpit.

a.   *The Agonizer.* This is the member of the Pew who is known by practically every active member of the congregation. Agonizer is known as an attacker. His or her tongue is as sharp as a sword. For Pulpit, if for no other, Agonizer is evidence of the truth in James' words, namely, "but no one can tame the tongue, a restless evil full of deadly poison" *(Jas. 3:8).* I said, "if for no other," because Agonizer functions with the expressed or the unexpressed sanctions of other members. Silence indeed gives consent.

In congregational business meetings, Agonizer is something of a loose cannon. That is the setting in which Agonizer is most active. The involvement begins after the reading of the minutes. Usually, the secretary is accused of missing something Agonizer claims to have said, or of missing a motion Agonizer claimed to have made or seconded.

Agonizer is a stickler for correctness in parliamentary procedure. Pulpit as chair of the meeting is the target of those inquiries. Efforts may be made to embarrass or to show up Pulpit. If there are no avenues of entry for Agonizer through parliamentary rules, the agenda is questioned. Agonizer may charge Pulpit with having a closed agenda. Even Pulpit's explanations to the effect that there is an established date for getting items on the agenda, or to the effect that as chairperson time is needed to prepare for discussions on agenda items, Agonizer lets Pulpit know that the Church is the Pew. And to make it clear that Agonizer may be a self-appointed spokesperson, but one, nonetheless, people sanctioned, a statement such as, "And we have the right to make up the agenda. It is our church." Pulpit is portrayed as a dictator, if not a tyrant.

Agonizer is a very active participant in the congregation's business meeting. He or she makes an issue out of non-essential matters. Often meetings are prolonged and dragged out by one person. Occasionally while in an attack mode Agonizer may chastise others while attacking Pulpit, by saying, "You all sit here and act like you are scared. Then, after the meeting you call me telling me what I said needed to be said."

Without doubt Agonizer can cause Pulpit some anxiety and for some others of the Pew, Agonizer intimidates them. So how does Pulpit respond to Agonizer?

Pulpit is tempted, I am sure, to strike back. But rarely if ever does the one in charge win a battle by fighting fire with fire. So, what do you do? Do you treat Agonizer with kindness, thereby, heaping coals of fire upon the head? *(cf. Rom. 12:17-21)*. Whether kindness does or does not convert Agonizer it must be done, nonetheless.

Why not evaluate Agonizer's role, first? Maybe he or she plays an invaluable role in the congregation. Agonizer, though annoying, may be just the gadfly Pulpit needs. Whether Pulpit admits it or not, sometimes without outside prodding, programs lose their sharpness, meetings lose purpose and focus. Even an impatient group in church business meetings may learn to appreciate Agonizer with some help and guidance from Pulpit. Agonizer is not a person who is permanently hostile or evil. He or she has an understanding of self as a champion of the people's causes and rights and feels a sense of calling to protect and preserve them. Once Pulpit understands Agonizer in that light it may be possible to engage him or her by seeking out their counsel and advice on pertinent matters. By all means, Pulpit must neither attack nor publicly appease Agonizer. Attack will strengthen Agonizer's position as other members sympathize with him or her. They may see powerful Pulpit picking on one little church member. Appeasement will only serve to anger Agonizer for it will appear as though Pulpit is looking down on him or her. Pulpit becomes, therefore, a condescender. Best of all, I believe, is an approach that leaves Agonizer's proud role intact even though it may be a bit more structured and conforming.[27] Accomplishing that feat means that Pulpit will treat Agonizer with respect, tolerate his or her attacks, acknowledge the presentation, move and wait. If other members tire of the outbursts and feel a slaying is in order

---

[27]cf. Carl S. Dudley, "Me and Mrs. Jones," *The Christian Ministry*, May-June 1996, p. 9.

they will do it. If a wounding of Agonizer's self pride is what they feel is justified, they will do that, also.

    b.   *The Signifier.* Where I grew up, Hoffman, North Carolina, we had a saying, "Signifying is worse than stealing." Dr. Charles H. Long in his book, *Significations, Signs, Symbols, and Images in the Interpretation of Religion* says he learned as a boy in Little Rock, Arkansas that, "Signifying is worse that lying." He says the reason why is "because it *(signifying)* obscures and obfuscates a discourse without taking responsibility for so doing."[28]

    Professor Long says, "Signifying is a very clever language game." A pastor invited a friend to preach to his congregation. At the conclusion of the sermon when the invitation to discipleship was extended, seventeen persons offered themselves for church membership. At the close of the service as the pastor stood on the door greeting worshippers, Signifier looked at him with a big smile on his face. He sided up to his ear and whispered, "I've never seen that many persons join a church at one time. Maybe you ought to have him back next Sunday."

---

[28] _____ (Philadelphia, Fortress Press, 1986), p. 1.

Much later, Pulpit visited Signifier while he was a patient in the hospital. During that year at least one person joined the church for forty one consecutive Sundays. Then, for the three Sundays prior to him entering the hospital no one joined. Signifier was in the patients lounge on his floor of the hospital. Immediately after their mutual greetings he said, "Reverend, what's happening? We aren't taking anybody in the church."

Signifier knew how much Pulpit tried to provide leadership in church administration. It was a ministry that he felt the Spirit gifted him *(cf. I Cor. 12:28 NKJV)*. Invariably, Signifier would drop into Pulpit's office and advise him on the need to "run the Church like a business." Much to Pulpit's chagrin, he thought that we were applying and following good administrative principles. Of course, Pulpit learned that Signifier had nothing to contribute to what running the church like a business meant. He had watched and observed, listened and studied Pulpit enough to know some things about him. Pulpit expected persons to join the church every Sunday, after preaching a sermon. That passion was stimulated by what happened after Peter's Pentecost sermon. The people were cut to the heart and they said to Peter and the other apostles, "Brothers, what should we do?" *(cf. Acts 2:37-39)*

Signifier knew, also, that Pulpit was proud of the manner in which the affairs of the congregation were administered. He regarded the whole, or the entire operations as administration. But the daily operations operated smoothly. Though Signifier was an officer of the congregation he was not interested in the proper working of every part. His one and only interest was money which was outside of the responsibilities of the Board he served on. His interest in money was limited to his feeling that if everybody paid a share some could pay less. He had no appreciation for the teaching, "From everyone to whom much has been given, much will be required; and from the one to whom much has been entrusted, even more will be demanded" *(Lk. 12:48)*.

Signifier knows how to get Pulpit's goat. Getting under Pulpit's skin is an avocation of Signifier. Pulpit felt his preaching gift was weak. Signifier knew how deficient he felt in the preaching ministry. He signified often, negatively addressing the pastor's poor pulpit performance by building him up, comparing him and placing him on the same plateau with some outstanding pulpiteers. He might say, "I don't know what you are talking about. You preach as good as Dr. Gospel Baptist."

How do you deal with Signifier? It might not be such a problem if Pulpit did not have such an insatiable appetite for acceptance. Signifier comes across as being in the, "I don't really care for you" column. Signifier's non-acceptance of Pulpit puts a bad mark on Pulpit's popularity rating. Pulpit would rather be right than popular, right? Jesus taught, "Woe to you when all speak well of you, for that is what their ancestors did to the false prophets" *(Lk. 6:26)*. Yet, Pulpit as a class want acceptance and approval.

It might seem from what I have written that Pulpit has only one Signifier. By no means do I mean that. I used the one example to illustrate my points. Dealing with Signifier means acknowledging that the attacks are personal. Even when Pulpit is tempted to strike out at the Signifier, be constrained by what is best in the long run. "For it is God's will that you should silence the ignorance of the foolish" *(I Pet. 2:15)*. To silence the Signifier means enduring some potshots at Pulpit's pride. Beyond the personal pride Pulpit must strive for what is right. That is, right in terms of motives for actions; right in terms of the choices made on which actions are based; and right in terms of the means employed in fulfilling and reaching the ends toward which the choices lead.... "If you endure when you do right and suffer for it, you have God's approval" *(I Pet. 2:20b)*. I am not attempting to make a martyr of Pulpit. My aim is to steer away from self-righteousness by suggesting that it is the responsibility of Pulpit to seek for righteousness that is of God. Which means that as far as anyone is humanly able, including Pulpit, they must deny themselves and take up their cross and follow Christ *(cf. Matt. 16:24-26)*. In this way when attacks come, Pulpit is ever closer to keeping the exhortation of Peter. Namely, "Keep your conscience clear, so that, when you are maligned, those who abuse you for your good conduct in Christ may be put to shame" *(I Pet. 3:16)*.

Pulpit must never allow Agonizer or Signifier to get their dander up to the point where the pulpit is used to take potshots at them. To do so would be to take unfair advantage since preaching is not really dialogic. Therefore, Pew cannot talk back at Pulpit.

Also, Pulpit takes chances by talking to other members critically about antagonist. As far as it is possible to do so, talk one on one with Agonizer and Signifier. When talking with others about them, as far as it is possible, build them up. Pulpit must practice and teach others, "to speak evil of no one, to avoid quarreling, to be gentle, and to show every courtesy to everyone" *(Titus 3:2)*.

If all possible, Pulpit must not permit Signifier to succeed in causing him or her to strike back. But I also feel that in some instances Signifier may be disarmed by Pulpit bringing to his or her mid what he or she is doing and how it affects Pulpit. Sometimes an individual may not be conscious of the frequency of the annoyances.

     c.   *The Hypocrite.*   I suspect that every congregation has a Hypocrite, one or more. Hypocrite's tactics are divisive. Pulpit who has experienced Hypocrite knows the deviousness of the tactics. They follow two approaches. One, Hypocrite uses both faces related to a financial rally, drive, or big day. Pulpit is depending on the outcome of the effort to meet a major obligation. Let me make it clear that the most harmful Hypocrite is the more powerful member of the congregation, or Pew. Pulpit may turn to such a member before undertaking a major financial effort. At that point, and if not at that point, some other, Hypocrite commits to the effort. Pulpit is under the impression that Hypocrite is on board. That lifts the spirit and inspires the hope of Pulpit. Hypocrite's cooperative face has a smile and a countenance that assures and reassures. Indeed, Pulpit is encouraged and inspired.

Hypocrite by interpretation has another face. The promise to support "the program" is a facade. That is made evident when Hypocrite gets on the telephone, or in private conversations and talks down the ensuing activity. Key persons are contacted along with Pulpit's known opposition. Success is not measured by total failure of the effort. It is measured by falling substantially below the set goal. Hypocrite knows how to play the game well. Not only does he or she pledge program support to Pulpit but also pays his or her "asking for the Rally" to Pulpit. What more confirmation of commitment and support is necessary?

Hypocrite has another method of operation. The business meeting of the congregation approaches. Pulpit has a pet project in mind, which is revealed to a few key leaders. They discuss it and say they like it. They think it will go over. However, no explicit pledge of support is asked or given. Based on the nature of the discussion and the consensus that "it will work," a pledge of support was Pulpit's assumption and conclusion.

Pulpit's assumption was short-lived. Once the proposal was presented it began to be discussed. That was not a bad thing. In fact it was a healthy sign. It was an indication to Pulpit of members maturing and once the proposal if it was adopted they would have bought into it, rather than adopting it uncritically. But, as the discussion continued it became clear to Pulpit that something was wrong. The dominant voice among "the key leaders" was deafingly silent. Pulpit began to sense having been had, or having been set up. Rather than lose everything Pulpit recommends putting the issue on the table. It was.

After the meeting closed and the congratulations on a good meeting and the condolences over the tabled matter had drawn to a close, Hypocrite came like Nicodemus, so to speak, "by night" *(cf. John 3:2)*. I use "by night" to mean "in secret," or under "the cloak of secrecy." Hypocrite sided up to Pulpit and quietly expressed regret over the failure of Pulpit's proposal and, in what seemed like the same breath, attempted to reassure Pulpit where Hypocrite stood on the matter. Hypocrite said, "Pastor, I want you to know I was with you in there." Pulpit replied with a simple, "Thank you."

Hypocrite is a difficult type adversary to confront. However, I mentioned already that when Paul found Cephas acting, or behaving hypocritically, he wrote, "But when Cephas came to Antioch, I opposed him to his face, because he stood self-condemned" *(Gal. 2:11)*. Yet, it is not easy for Pulpit to confront Hypocrite in such a personal and direct way. Paul and Cephas were equals. They were both apostles *(cf. Gal. 2:6-10)*. Pulpit and Pew share an equality in Christ. Yet, within the church they share an inequality based on functions. That inequality is compounded by a paradox of Pulpit being in charge, on the one hand, and being financially dependent on Pew, on the other hand. Direct confrontation may not always be the best approach.

How should Pulpit deal with Hypocrite? I am not sure that there is one approach that works in every instance. A wise Pulpit seeks to know key leaders in the pew. What makes them behave hypocritically differ from individual to individual. Pew in one instance may need personal attention. That information may come to Pulpit from a confidante. Every individual who pastors ought to cultivate relationships with a few select members who provide information on what makes Hypocrite tick. Pulpit might learn from information received that Hypocrite is disturbed by Pulpit's lack of a show of attention. Such attention had always been lavished upon Hypocrite until this Pulpit came. So, Pulpit might be able to make a few telephone calls and bring about a transformation in Hypocrite. Even a little more intentional attention directed towards Hypocrite may result in change.

Also, Hypocrite may act in what appears to be a treacherous manner feeling left out of the power loop. Attempting to persuade Pulpit of being happy and content, Hypocrite is friendly, always appearing cordial and cooperative. Beneath the tranquil surface, however, is a malcontent, seething like a volcano waiting to erupt. Having been in the power loop, Pew is not comfortable out of it. When a Pharaoh comes to the seat of power who does not know Joseph *(cf. Exod. 1:8)*, an uncomfortable situation is created for Joseph. Joseph may respond in different ways to his new environment. He may "fold his tent like an Arab, and silently steal away." Or, Joseph may go underground and from that position work to bring Pulpit down. Or, Hypocrite may pretend not to be bothered by being out of the loop and put up a good front. From that posture Hypocrite stages two-faced attacks. At the base of the attacks is anger over the loss of power.

Pulpit may ignore Hypocrite, provided enough support is garnered from the Pew to move on. After all, not every malcontent and not every discontent should be appeased, nor brought back into the power loop. That is a call Pulpit should make and suffer it to be so if Hypocrite is to remain outside of the loop.

Pulpit may conference with Hypocrite. In that session, Hypocrite may be told that for now Pulpit is sharing power with more individuals in order to broaden the base of leadership. Hypocrite may or may not be promised a place but what should be made clear, provided it is consistent with Pulpit's leadership philosophy, is that a democratic style will prevail. And those who broker power must be both responsible and accountable to the congregation.

Paul dressed Cephas down "before them all." His approach, however, was of such that the onus was placed on Cephas. He did not simply approach Cephas to his face, he ended this phase with a question which turned the matter back on him. Paul asked Cephas, "If you, though a Jew, live like a Gentile and not like a Jew, how can you compel the Gentiles to live like Jews?" *(Gal. 2:14)*

This is a reasoned approach. But should Pulpit use it to counter or to transform Pew, it must be remembered that Paul wrote with Cephas' prior commitment in mind. In a sense, this was an appeal to Cephas' conscience. He had made much to do of his vision on Simon the tanner's roof top in Joppa. He told the Church in Jerusalem of the subsequent experience at Cornelius' house in Caesarea, where the Holy Spirit fell on Gentiles while he was still speaking *(cf. Acts 10:11-18)*. Should Pew approach Hypocrite with reasoning, appeal must be made using the prior vow of Church membership. What was at stake for Cephas was his word, the same is so in the case of Hypocrite. Ultimately, the appeal is to the conscience.

In conflict situations Christians must not neglect the redeemed goodness in their brothers and sisters in Christ. The presence and power of the Holy Spirit should not be played cheap. He moves yet according to his own volition. For the baptized the Holy Spirit is within and may move, even in Hypocrite to convict of wrong doing and of deviant behavior, thus, leading to repentance. That should be more important to Pulpit than holding on to animosity toward Hypocrite.

    d.   The Character. Character is the loud mouthed, unrestrained church member who feels free to say what he or she desires to say. Character laughs a lot, jokes a lot, caustically, however, and directs much of her remarks toward Pulpit's spouse and children. Given the way others of the Pew laugh and try without much effort and energy to restrain Character, they approve. If so they are not the first to express their mean spirit through another. One has to wonder, however, who would delight in mistreating Pew's family. Even when as I suspect the ultimate target is Pulpit. To go through Pulpit's family is cowardice. But cowardice is one of the characteristics of Character. It is cowardice even though the attack on Pulpit is indirect. To engage in missile strikes on the Pastor by attacking the spouse and children border on cowardly behavior. A worthy husband, wife, or parent will feel the hurt that is inflicted on any other family member.

Character may use the telephone to harass Pulpit's spouse on matters for which she or he has no responsibility, and likely no knowledge as well. Given the opportunity, Character will make some calls at the most inopportune times, at meal time, or when getting the children ready for bed.

Character may engage Pulpit's spouse acting as a fashion consultant. "Honey, that does not go with that." The "thats" may be a hat, a blouse, shoes, a jacket, or a skirt. Any garment, apparel, or accessory will do as a target of attack for Character.

Character may engage Pulpit's spouse suggesting bad taste. "Child, I know you're young, but a preacher's wife ain't got no business wearing a dress that short. Did your husband see you before you left home? Did he let you come out looking like that?"

An African proverb says, "It takes a village to raise a child." When it comes to Pulpit's child, or children,

Character tries to be the whole village. Pulpit's children can never do anything right. They look terrible no matter what they have on. Character thinks nothing of asking, "Baby, who dressed you?" "I know your mama didn't put that on you." "Come here, baby, let me fix your hair. You are too pretty a child to look like that!"

Pulpit's spouse owes it to her own mental health not to allow Character to cause her to be hospitalized. So, what should she do? She should tell Character that enough is enough, and enough does not mean "More." She must get Character off her back. In doing so strained relationships may result. Pulpit will be included but for the sake of Pulpit's family well-being strained relationships is a small price to pay. Yet, it is encumbent upon Pulpit to show love toward Character. With her off the backs of the children, they may need help in understanding why Character no longer gives them attention. With the attention in words were small favors, like candy and cookies. But in the final analysis the children are better off without Character and so are Pulpit and spouse. Character is a mental, spiritual and physical drain on Pulpit and family.

e. *The Reminder.* Pulpit in a new congregation, except as organizer, is subject to being reminded of predecessors. In one area or another of predecessors ministries Pulpit will be confronted by the Reminder. Having followed a very well beloved and highly respected Pastor in one pastorate, I encountered the Reminder in several degrees. I visited an elderly member who was a patient in the hospital, and met immediate rejection. As soon as I entered the room, the patient began a chant, saying, "I love X. I love X." Needless to say I was temporarily knocked for a loop. I had never laid eyes on that member before that day.

My predecessor was a great preacher, I felt. I was congratulated in the early months after each Sunday worship service by Reminder with such kind words as, "A good speech, Reverend," or, "A fine address."

Reminder may use a plethora of things predecessors did differently and better than Pulpit. But there is another side that is also difficult for Pulpit with integrity to deal with. Reminder may be a predecessor downer. There is a saying in some church circles that say, "The best pastors a congregation can have are the one it just had and the one it will get, next." Reminder attempts to break down the truth of the saying by playing up to Pulpit, while putting down the immediate predecessor. Reminder creates a temptation for Pulpit.

Reminder is a genius also, at reminding Pulpit that he or she knows "these people" in ways that Pulpit does not. Unless Pulpit remains alert and is careful not to be overly influenced by Reminder, "these people," and especially the individuals named will not receive an objective assessment by Pulpit, nor will they receive opportunities to relate to their Pastor without prejudice, or pre-judgment. In a word, Reminder's attempts to use Pulpit's ignorance of the membership may be blatant efforts to position oneself as Pulpit's confidante. At the same time while narrowing Pulpit's relationship base Reminder moves in as a gullible Pulpit's sole friend. But to the wise Pulpit, the motive for doing so should always be held suspect.

Reminder annoyed me reminding me of what I had not done. He or she was adept at not only locating sick or shut-in members, but of asking, "Has the Pastor been to see you?" Some of the recently found members had been away from church for months, or for years. I thought a fair way for Reminder to operate would have been to ask the member, "When were you last in church?" But that question did not square with Reminder's intention, which was to antagonize Pulpit. Another thing that fit well into Reminder's intention was to remind Pulpit that, "It seems like attendance at the Sunday services has fallen off." Anything that pointed to failure on Pulpit's part, or that reflected negatively on Pulpit's ministry was brought up. Reminder is a specialist in reminding and is an expert in hitting Pulpit where it hurts most. It might be that Pulpit seems to have an obsession with success. Maybe its in the genes of the Spirit's gift to pastors.

Pulpit has to bear some burdens. Reminder may be one of them. Though it might appear, to some, that Reminder plays a helpful part. It could be true if it were not for the attitude, demeanor and the approach used by Reminder. Most in the Pulpit class would welcome someone who serves in a positive role as Reminder. That role is best served by a Reminder who asks or speaks before the fact. Negative Reminders kick up Pulpit's dander after the fact. At that point reminding is designed to reflect negatively on Pulpit.

f.   *Pulpit As The Enemy.* I will paraphrase the Peanuts character, "I found the enemy and it is I." Pulpit may be his or her own Enemy. It is the design of this section to specify possible manifestations of the Enemy.

Unpastoral Preaching. Let me get at this matter by saying that I describe pastoral preaching as the gospel directed to address the needs of members of the Pew. Pastors who sit where the people sit are uniquely positioned to preach pastorally. Nearly a century ago, Harry Emerson Fosdick told preachers to "begin with the real problems of the people. Every sermon should have for its main business the head-on-constructive meeting of some problem which (is) puzzling minds, burdening consciences, distracting lives."[29]

Preaching pastorally is possible only when pastors immerse themselves in the lives of those in the congregation who have "puzzling minds, burdening consciences, distracting lives." Without intimate knowledge of Pew, Pulpit will preach unpastorally. Preaching in that vein is no more than "detached, helpful,

---

[29]Quoted by William H. Willimon, "Pastoral Preaching," *The Christian Ministry*, Sept.-Oct. 1996, p. 16.

generic care."[30] Pulpit's calling to pastor embraces preaching that keeps our care *pastoral*. As Pulpit, "We are caring for people in the name of Christ, with reference to the traditions and witness of the church, in the context of the gathered congregation at worship--which makes the care given in a sermon uniquely Christian."[31]

Pastoral preaching in the context of the church gathered for worship proclaims the gospel in ways that answer the needs of worshippers. It interprets the nature and meaning of the church in ways that demands of worshippers behavior consistent with what it means to be Christian. Negative, disruptive, and antagonistic behavior may result from unrequited and unresolved guilt. Pastoral preaching does not lead to further entrenchment of guilt, it is directed instead towards the confession of sin and to repentance.

Pastoral preaching takes sin seriously but grace is taken more seriously. For sin is not grace's equal. There is no person, nor any problem in a congregation for which

---

[30]Ibid.

[31]Ibid.

grace does not have the capacity to change, or to solve. Where preaching is not pastoral, a climate conducive to growth and growing is not being cultivated. The gospel made relevant and applicable to the human predicament creates such a climate.

Losing The Cool. I have had persons approach me after a meeting and congratulate me on my calm handling of situations. I say, "Thank you!" while saying to myself, "If only you knew how tempted I was to let go all of my impatience and my frustration." If I do keep my cool it is the result of directed effort. I work at it because of my strong temper.

Anger expressed under certain circumstances and in certain situations play into the hands of Pew with provocative instincts. They set out in business meetings to make Pulpit lose it. And that is what happens, Pulpit loses it. Pulpit loses the war. Church members want Pulpit to remain in control of his or her anger when attacked. When the cool is lost, agitators win. For Pulpit descends to the level of the provokers. "One who is slow to anger is better than the mighty" *(Prov. 16:32).* "Do not be quick to anger, for anger lodges in the bosom of fools" *(Eccl. 7:9).* When

Pulpit shows anger, provokers capitalize on it. They dig around in it as one uses a stoker to dig around in coals of fire. In so doing anger fuels on anger.

To be a conqueror in circumstances in which individuals go after you, practice being cool and resolve to maintain your cool in spite of how difficult it may be to do so. I believe its true, "each victory will help you some others to win." Concentrate on how great the price for Pulpit to lose his or her cool.

Playing The Martyr. Pulpit may secretly love and cherish the darts that Pew throws and which pierce Pulpits heart, mind and spirit. It is not the hurt or the pain that Pulpit loves and cherishes. Rather, it is the consequence of what darts bring. One of my early pastoral mentors used to tell how he created stories and told them from the pulpit while shedding tears, just to gain sympathy and support of members. Following the benediction he told of how members came to him and asked, "Who is bothering you?" "What have they done to you?" My mentor's attacks were make believe. Some may even accuse him of a cruel hoax. Nonetheless, my mentor sought sympathy, support. He was not a true machoists who loved the pain.

What is wrong with Pulpit seeking sympathy and support? It might be argued that the means used don't justify the ends. It might be asked are the ends noble and good? Or, it might be asked, how may Pulpit know that by serving as a punching bag for Pew the desired ends will be realized? Therefore, even if the ends are noble and good the possibility exists that the means might taint them. Instead of sympathy and support the results might be pity. For pedagogical purposes only, pity is used here to refer to looking down on another. Pew may feel sorrow for Pulpit but in a manner of inequality. I maintain that Pew does not respect a pitied Pulpit. To lead a congregation, Pulpit needs to show strength. Pitifulness opens Pulpit up to references such as, "Our poor Pastor." Or, "He/she is a pathetic figure." Or, "He/she is a poor excuse for a Pastor."

What do I suggest? First and foremost, Pulpit will receive darts from the Pew. Authority figures attract attackers. Pain and grief go with Pulpit's territory. The fact that in local congregations Pulpit makes choices among persons means that some members are selected and some are not. Consequently, some are happy and others are sad, or some are mad. Maybe angry is a better word. Some angry people fight back. They hurl brickbats. They throw darts.

Also, Pulpit stands before the congregation Sunday after Sunday and preaches the gospel of Christ. The fact of standing as a peculiar spokesperson for God incurs wrath and jealousy. It was mentioned earlier how Miriam and Aaron expressed jealousy toward Moses. They asked, "Has the Lord spoken only through Moses? Has he not spoken through us also?" *(Numb. 8:2)*. Pew might feel that Pulpit can't tell him or her anything, because he or she hears from God, too. The Lord acknowledged to Miriam and Aaron that he does reveal Himself to others, but there are differences between the methods He uses. He said,

> *Hear my words: When there are prophets among you, I the Lord make myself known to them in visions; I speak to them in dreams.*
>
> *Not so with my servant Moses; he is entrusted with all my house.*
>
> *With him I speak face to face--clearly, not in riddles; and he behold the form of the Lord.*
> Numb. 12:6-8

Pulpit has no need to pretend that persecution is being experienced. A persecution complex may not be the best piece of equipment for Pulpit. Since pain and grief go with the territory two things should be developed. Lest Pulpit responds to suffering by becoming revengeful, mean and conniving, a thick skin must be grown. It is a garment that will be needed again and again. One that protects against what Paul called, "the flaming arrows of the evil one" *(Eph. 6:16)*. His thick skin, he called, "the shield of faith" *(16a)*.

The other piece of equipment is a theology of suffering, which is the belief that under the proper conditions suffering can mean something. Proper conditions include *doing right* *(I Pet. 2:20b)*. Which is the normal behavior for those whose *being is right* *(I Pet. 1:3)*. Suffering reveals God's approval *(I Pet. 2:20)*. It accrues to the genuineness of Pulpit's faith "and may be found to result in praise and glory and honor when Christ Jesus is revealed" *(I Pet. 1:7)*. In all instances of suffering Pulpit needs to be careful to be in the will of God. Attacks endured for doing wrong do not work to the growth of Pulpit, neither is Christ glorified by them.

Lacking A Sense of Humor. In one of the churches I pastored, a woman said to me one day, "There is nothing wrong with you that a good laugh won't cure." What she had observed was an unsmiling Pastor. I grew up at a time when Pulpit exemplified a serious demeanor. Preachers wore colors of black, blue, and gray. In fact, in the same city, my physician said to me, "Maybe if you lighten the colors in your wardrobe, you might brighten up your personality."

What I gathered from what the two persons said was I lacked a sense of humor. "The real essence of humor, after all, has to do with perspective. The word is from the Latin *humis*, "of the earth." Comedy has always been concerned with bringing people back to earth and reminding them of their humanity. As such, it is godly, and worth cultivating in the church."[32]

Jesus showed humor when he sent a message by the Pharisees to Herod, saying, "Go and tell that fox for me, ..." *(Lk. 13:32).* By using "that fox" to refer to Herod, Jesus

---

[32]John Killinger. "How I Slayed Bullies, Ghosts and Other Tormentors," *The Christian Ministry*, May-June 1996, p. 26.

let it be known that Herod was not strong and all powerful. Rather, he was "a cunning but weak ruler."[33]

The apostle Paul must have had a sense of humor. Remember what he said about the Galatian Christians who were undermining his ministry and insisting that people must be circumcised into Judaism before becoming Christians? It was something like: "I hope their precious knives slip and they castrate themselves."[34]

Humor brings Pulpit and Pew down to earth. Individuals who are able to laugh at themselves are less likely to think more highly of themselves than they ought to think *(Rom. 12:3)*.

Pulpit becomes a lightning rod for Pew, sometimes, because humility is lacking. Without humility, arrogance creeps in. Arrogance travels on the vehicle called, "Reverend." As soon as some preachers are licensed, but without orders, they become, "Reverend." With the laying

---

[33]*The New International Commentary On The New Testament, The Gospel of Luke* (Wm. B. Eerdmans Publishing Co., Grand Rapids, Mich., 1951), p. 382.

[34]Killenger, op. cit., p. 26.

on of hands some preachers get "the big head," which is nothing more than an attitude that makes it difficult to work with others. A big part of pastoring is relating to others. Even when I spoke of inequality of functions, I maintained there is equality of all who are in Christ *(Gal. 3:28)*. An attitude that sends a signal that Pulpit feels superior attracts negative reactions. Pulpit to whom Pew looks for a word from the Lord should learn from Christ whose exaltation was the direct consequence of humility that allowed him to endure humiliation *(Philp. 2:5-11)*. Humility is not weakness. It is to relinquish status for the sake of Christ that through our service to others he may be glorified. When Pulpit becomes humble, Christ is lifted up. John the Baptist said it best, "He must increase, but I must decrease" *(John 3:30)*.

When Pew looks at Pulpit his or her perception is important. It is true that some will dislike Pulpit for no reason at all. There are others who will relate according to the image Pulpit displays among the people.

Un-loving. Many years ago my wife asked a relative how she liked her pastor. That inquiry was made after Pulpit had been on the charge for several years. Her relative said, "We found out his smile is not for real." Her terse statement said in effect that Pulpit was phony, he pretended to care for Pew, but he did not. I contend that Pulpit cannot get along for very long faking love. Love has one source, God. He is reality and has no part in fakery and fraudulent behavior. Consequently, Pulpit's attempts to fake love will be exposed. "For there is nothing hidden, except to be disclosed; nor is anything secret, except to come to light" *(Mk. 4:22)*.

Because love is of God *(I John 5:8)*, all who love God love one another *(cf. I John 4:7-12)*. Pulpit is called by God in Christ to represent Him to Pew and to represent Pew before Himself. Through the proclamation of the Word of God Pulpit is the Lord's voice to His people. Through the pastoral prayer with the congregation assembled Pulpit represents the people before God. Pulpit ought to image God's love to the people in assembly. That is best done when Pew knows of Pulpit's love for the people. While there may always be a few enemies in the Pew where people receive love from Pulpit love is given in return. Love is more than words. "Little children, let us love, not in word or speech, but in truth and action" *(I John 3:18)*.

In congregations where the word is circulated on Pulpit, which says in essence, "That preacher don't care a thing about us," open season on Pulpit is declared. Support for the claim comes in specifics such as, "He doesn't visit the sick." Or, "I was in the hospital for three weeks and she didn't visit me one time." "When my Mama died, Pulpit never even called to say, "I'm sorry. He could have picked up the telephone and called."

Being a loving pastor does not mean being a doormat. Love itself has a tough side. Pew accepts that side when he and she are conditioned by Pulpit's expression of love's tender side. When people are confident their pastor loves them they accept exhortation, reproof, and chastisement. It is like our parents used to say to us just before administering a spanking, or, was it a whipping? They would say, "I am doing this because I love you." And because of their prior actions on our behalf their spankings were accepted as discipline and not as abuse. So when Pulpit administers a verbal spanking through the proclamation of the gospel where love has been demonstrated Pew receives it as discipline in the faith.

Double-minded. Pulpit is called to lead. Double mindedness is a blight on leadership. According to the apostle James, it is symptomatic of "the doubter," who is also "unstable in every way" *(Jas. 1:8)*, Pulpit who is double minded will anguish in poverty of spiritual things. For, he or she "must not expect to receive anything from the Lord" *(Jas. 1:8)*. Without receiving from the Lord spiritual blessings which Pulpit would share, Pew becomes spiritually depleted. Without the Spirit's active presence in the life of the congregation the people become ripe for behavior uncharacteristic of Christians.

Pulpit with a double mind is like a bugler whose bugle gives an indistinct sound. Paul asked, "And if the bugle gives an indistinct sound, who will get ready for battle?" *(I Cor. 14:8)*. The people look to Pulpit for clear direction. Without spiritual direction a congregation may become guilty of the condition Israel got in. Deuteronomy 12:8 puts the condition, thus; "You shall not act as we are acting here today, all of us according to our own desires."

I liken what is described here to a state of lawlessness. John the apostle said, "sin is lawlessness" *(I John 3:4b)*.

Without direction, Pew is in a state of wandering. The state is not unlike that Moses sought to have Pharaoh believe Israel was in just after they fled Egypt. Moses gave orders for the people to turn back in order to make Pharaoh think the Israelites "are wandering aimlessly in the land; the wilderness has closed in on them" *(Exod. 14:3)*. Unfortunately, a congregation led by a double minded pulpit may "wander aimlessly." As its members are swallowed up by" confusion and chaos brought on as the consequence of individuals acting according to their own desires, Pulpit may become the major target of Pew's attacks. Pulpit will be the focus of the cries, "we have no leadership." It is easy to say that each member ought to be held personally responsible for participation in collective confusion. That charge is indisputable. However, a lack of community which contributes in every instance to collective chaos leads to the door of Pulpit's study. Pulpit is never blameless if he or she has been at the head of a congregation for long enough time to focus the gospel message of unity, oneness and love upon the membership.

Jesus had an eye for sheep who were in trouble. Mark's Gospel paints a portrait of Jesus being briefed by his disciples, they "told him all they had done and taught" *(Mk. 6:30)*. Jesus saw all of the people coming and going, so he said to the twelve, "Come away to a desert place all by yourselves and rest awhile" *(31)*. "They went away in a boat to a deserted place by themselves" *(32)*. It was impossible, it appears, for Jesus and his disciples, to get away. When the crowd recognized the entourage they followed on foot. Mark wrote of Jesus' assessment of what he saw as he went ashore. He wrote, "he saw a great crowd; and he had compassion for them, because they were like sheep without a shepherd..." *(34a)*.

Jesus did two things. I mention this because of the wandering spirit of congregations which compares with sheep without a shepherd. And because of what Jesus did to minister to their needs, which if done by Pulpit will prevent confusion, or will provide curative measures for confused memberships. First, Jesus "began to teach them" *(34b)*, which suggests that he provided for their spiritual needs. Instruction in things spiritual enlightens regarding the nature, meaning and mission of the church and the duties and responsibilities of members.

Second, Jesus provided for the physical needs of the sheep without a shepherd. Doing so he also provided structure for them. He had his disciples to instruct the people to sit down in groups *(cf. Mk. 6:35-44)*. They did so. From that point the people looked like sheep with a shepherd. Pulpit is expected to offer food for the total being of Pew. Where this is done there is a sense of order and orderliness in the congregation. Without order and discipline, responsibility and accountability in a congregation, Pulpit may be the target of abuse. Pew will take out frustration on the person expected to lead.

Not Preaching. There is a saying in African American churches that goes like this: "People will forgive a preacher for everything, except for not preaching." Unfortunately, in many instances preaching is more sound than substance. Regardless of the meaning of preaching held by those who utter the saying referenced above, I have included it under the Enemy umbrella because of its role in community making and maintenance. Where the Word is not preached, people may feel they have a license to do as everyone desires. The Word preached is community creating. For it is not preaching about *Christ*. Rather, the content of preaching *is Christ*. In the synagogue in Thessalonica on the Sabbath, Paul "reasoned with them from the Scriptures, explaining and demonstrating "that the Christ had to suffer and rise again from the dead, and saying, "This Jesus whom I preach to you is the Christ" *(Acts 17:2-3 NKJV)*. Where Christ is preached the message demonstrates unity, for Christ is not divided *(I Cor. 1:13)*.

A divided, split, chaotic congregation is like the Gerasene Demoniac. Jesus asked, "What is your name?" He answered, "My name is Legion; for we are many" *(Mk. 5:9)*. Preaching the Word effects the transformation in a congregation that Jesus' words effected in the demoniac. After "the unclean spirits" were exorcised from the man and the shepherds went into the city and the country spreading the news, the people who came out to see what it was that had happened, saw the demoniac sitting there with Jesus, "clothed in his right mind" *(cf. Mk. 5:14-15)*.

Pew will be divided on the gospel being preached. The demoniac asked Jesus, "What have you to do with me, Jesus, Son of the Most High God?" He asked the question after Jesus had commanded him, the evil spirit, to come out *(Mk. 5:7, 8)*. Under the circumstances, his question reminds me of a snake that continues to wriggle after he is in the throes of death. For every intent and purpose the demon like the snake was finished. Giving up was painful. So it is for a congregation in which the Word is preached. Some members like the undisciplined and uncontrollable life as did the demoniac *(cf. Mk. 5:1-5)*. But it is life among the tombs *(2)*. That is where the dead are and in the Pew it is where the living dead are. But it is not life as God wills it. It leaves members restless and unfulfilled. Such a state and congregational condition will continue without the Word preached and empowered by the Spirit to give life. In such an environment, controversies, quarrels and divisions grow.

EPILOGUE

Pulpit is not one. Pulpit is a variety with differences of abilities, strengths and weaknesses. All in the class share common callings. They share a personal call. I like Luke's description of the calling of John the Baptist.

> *"In the fifteenth year of the reign of Emperor Tiberius, when Pontius Pilate was governor of Judea, and Herod was ruler of Galilee, and his brother Philip ruler of the region of Ituraea and Trachonitis, and Lysanias ruler of Abilene, during the high priesthood of Annas and Caiaphas, the word of God came to John son of Zechariah in the wilderness. "*
> Lk. 3:1-2

In the midst of the political reality and the religious reality, both of which are described by Luke, "the word of God came to John." It was not delivered to the palaces of the political rulers. Neither was it delivered to the religious leaders in the temple. It was delivered, instead, to an ascetic named John, "who was clothed with camel's hair, with a leather belt around his waist, and he ate locusts and wild honey" *(Mk. 1:6)*. "The word of God came to John son of Zechariah in the wilderness" *(Lk. 3:2b)*.

The symbolism in John's call must not go un-noticed. As I stated earlier in this section, God's word was not delivered to the politically powerful, nor to the religious leadership, which suggest to me that by entrusting His Word to John, a marginal figure, who as representative of Pulpit, forever set the inspired Word above every other reality.   King Zedekiah evidenced an awareness before John's time that God has a class of individuals into whose ears He whispers.   The King sent and had Jeremiah brought to his house, where he questioned him secretly. He asked the prophet, "Is there any word from the Lord?" Jeremiah said, "There is" *(Jer. 37:17)*.

There are differences among those who are in the Pulpit class.   But they are the ones set apart by God to receive and to proclaim His Word.   So, Pulpit is set apart by God's call to exercise peculiar functions.   Today, we refer to this calling as minister of Word, Sacraments and Discipline.   It is the calling central to the good health, the wholeness, and the welfare and well-being of the congregation.   So, Pulpit's calling is personal.   But it is also institutional.

It is institutional in the sense that an individual's claim to having been called comes under the scrutiny and judgment of the church or the denomination to which the individual belongs. In my denomination, the Christian Methodist Episcopal Church, the institutional call does not mean that by denying individuals opportunities to exercise their callings in it, the call has not been received. It means that according to its requirements, expectations, polity and doctrine some individuals are not suitable candidates for doing ministry in this denomination. Those who are called, and their call confirmed by this denomination, have hands laid on them and they are sent, in the tradition of Jesus sending his disciples *(John 17:18)*. They become the Pulpit about whom I have written. In the contexts to which they are sent to serve, they are positioned to provide leadership in the ministry of community building. Pulpit by his or her own leadership will serve the needs of community, and will work to overcome conflict, chaos and confusion, in order that community may be affirmed, flourish and grow.

Pew is the people. The people are the one body with many members. They, like Pulpit, bring to the transformed life human baggage, remnants of the unredeemed life. All things are new in principle, for those who are in Christ, but all things are not new, in fact. The saved by grace are in transition. God is working in them, gradually sanctifying all that was not immediately sanctified, set apart and made holy, through the new birth. While God with our cooperation is making us whole, we find ourselves answering another voice and call. Like our parents Adam and Eve we follow the voice of the serpent. Doing so we work against God's plan for community. We participate in divisive thinking, talking and walking that wreak havoc in the congregation.

We participate as individuals, as interest groups, as families, all in opposition to other individuals, interest groups, and families. Often Pulpit is pulled, even suckered into the middle of these intra-church feuds, fusses, and fights. Unwittingly, Pulpit may take side and end up in the middle getting slam dunked, bruised and battered. Yet, Pulpit is expected to negotiate or mediate the situation in spite of being victimized. This cannot be done by Pulpit alone. Peace, harmony and good will in a congregation are qualities for which all are called to preserve and protect. They belong with community and anyone who damages or destroys them are of the anti-Christ. For Christ is the embodiment of community.

Pew must know what the Church is, its nature, meaning, and mission. Pew must understand what it means to be a church member and to be one as a Christian. Pew must have an enlightened concept of Christianity, a personal religion, that is never private, but ever social. With Pulpit, Pew is reminded, that, "whenever we have an opportunity, let us work for the good of all, and especially for those of the family of faith" *(Eph. 6:10)*.

Pew is not called to confusion but to the ministry of peace. Following their Savior and Lord, Jesus the Christ, who "is our peace" they must keep down and not build up "the dividing wall, that is, the hostility between us" *(cf. Eph. 2:13, 14)*. No matter who participates in keeping alive long standing feuds, or who creates new ones, Pulpit must preach the gospel of peace. And remind all, "Blessed are the peacemakers, for they will be called children of God" *(Matt. 5:9)*.

It is essential for all members to understand and to accept their responsibility for community. Given the reality of sin in all of us it is unrealistic to think that conflict will be absent among the people of God. I am of the opinion that Jesus accepted the potential for conflict in the Church. Why else did he arrange for resolving disagreements and for expelling the unrepentant? *(cf. Matt. 18:15-20)* Problematic are the members who take pride in "raising hell." Believe me, I have met some of the ones who seem to think it is a game. They wear their title with great pride and pleasure. It is not easy for Pulpit to break down that cherished pride, which in some congregations is bolstered, supported and affirmed by others in the membership. The objects of their resistance to cooperation is often the ecclesiastical system, or individuals in it, but it targets Pulpit who is the most immediate representative of the system. In such cases Pulpit may not have any verbal help among the members. Often "hellraisers" are among the ablest and more affluent members of a congregation. They have disciples. Those who do not favor what is taking place may be too afraid to speak out, or to stand up and vote. Thus, Pulpit's only ally is the Spirit. It has been said by some of Pulpit's colleagues, "There is nothing wrong with that congregation that a few Christian funerals will not solve." Of course, I am not wishing death upon members who do not understand that their behavior is childish, any more than I wish death for those who understand that God has not given us a spirit of fear *(II Tim. 1:7a NKJV)*. I pray that all of us will pray with purpose. Praying that God will deliver the congregation from its imprisonment to confrontation and conflict, obstinance and vile meaness.

At the same time Pulpit must stay the course, proclaiming the gospel, remaining personally circumspect, teaching the truths of the faith, praying constantly, and loving the enemies of peace. Pew with Pulpit must learn forgiveness and practice humility that repentance will not be something which they are too proud to do. Did not the Lord, the Creator, Redeemer, and Strengthener of creation, repent?

REFERENCES

Allen, Charles L. *Prayer Changes Things* (Westwood, N.J., Fleming H. Revell, 1969), p. 10.

Barth, Karl. *Prayer* (Westminster, Philadelphia, 1952), p. 20.

The Broadman Bible Commentary, Vol. 10 (Nashville: Broadman Press, 1970), p. 356.

Daily Study Bible Series, The Gospel of Luke, p. 54.

Dudley, Carl S. "Me and Mrs. Jones," *The Christian Ministry*, May-June 1996, p. 9.

The Expository Bible Commentary, Vol. 11 (Grand Rapids, MI: Zondervan, 1978), p. 291.

Foster, Richard J. *Celebration of Discipline* (San Francisco: Harper and Row, 1988), p. 33.

Gilmore, Marshall (Bishop) editor. *The Book of Ritual of the Christian Methodist Episcopal Church* (C.M.E. Publishing House, Memphis, 1995), p. 119.

Heschel, Abraham Joshua. *I Asked for Wonder* (N.Y. Crossroad Publishing Co., 1988), p. 28.

The Interpreter's Bible, Vol. 9 (New York: Abingdon, 1954), p. 211.

Killinger, John. "How I Slayed Bullies, Ghosts and Other Tormentors," *The Christian Ministry,* May-June 1996.

Lofton, Fred C. *When We Pray* (Elgin, IL: Progressive Baptist Publishing House, 1978). Preface.

Long, Charles H. (Dr.). *Significations, Signs, Symbols, and Images in the Interpretation of Religion* (Philadelphia, Fortress Press, 1986), p. 1.

Marty, Martin E. "Conflict and Conflict Resolution," *The Living Pulpit,* July - Sept. 1994, p. 12.

The New International Commentary On The New Testament, The Gospel of Luke (Wm. B. Eerdmans Publishing Co., Grand Rapids, Mich., 1951), p. 382.

N.T. Study Bible Romans-Corinthians (Springfield, MO, The Complete Biblical Library, 1989), p. 123.

Read, David H.C. "Conflict - From Local to the Cosmic," *The Living Pulpit,* July - Sept. 1994, p. 4.

Quoted by E. H. Robertson. *Man's Estimate of Man* (Richmond, VA: Muhlenberg, 1958), p. 11.

Quoted by Douglas V. Steere. *Dimensions of Prayer* (N.Y.: Harper and Row, 1963), p. 3.

Quoted by William H. Willimon. "Pastoral Preaching," *The Christian Ministry,* Sept.-Oct. 1996, p. 16.

Winter, Gibson. "America In Search Of Its Soul," *Theology Today* (Princeton, N.J., Jan. 1996, Vol. 4), p. 472.

Wyon, Olive. *Prayer* (Muhlenberg, Philadelphia, 1960), p. 16.

Zodhiates, Spiros. *A Richer Life For You in Christ* (Chattanooga, TN: AME Publishers, 1972), p. 18f.